Relational
PARENTING

Relational
PARENTING

ROSS CAMPBELL, M.D.

MOODY PRESS
CHICAGO

Library of Congress Cataloging-in-Publication Data

Campbell, Ross, 1936-
    Relational parenting : going beyond your child's behavior to meet their deepest needs/ Ross Campbell.
    p. cm.
  ISBN: 0-8024-6393-2 (trade paper)
  1. Parent and child. 2. Parenting. I. Title

HQ755.85.C353 2000
649´.1--dc21   99-058017

1 3 5 7 9 10 8 6 4 2
Printed in the United States of America

Contents

First Words
from Ross . . .

A nother book on parenting? We already have five!"
Is that what you said to yourself when you saw this
title?

Yes, this is another book on parenting, but it may be quite different from those on your bookshelf. In fact, it could offer you a compelling, clear choice about the way you interact with your children.

This book is for those of you who have a nagging feeling that the approach to parenting you have been using for years just hasn't worked as promised. Something has gone wrong, and you have no clue what it is, since those who prescribed the method aren't offering any answers to why it hasn't worked. It is also for you parents of young children who hope to avoid some of the problems you see in other families.

As we begin a new century—and a new millennium—a rapidly changing world contributes to the growing numbers of difficulties our children encounter. Many of these children are from the best of homes and have wonderful Christian parents. Yet those parents don't understand what has happened to their once perfect families.

Let me give you some clues as to what may have gone wrong—clues we will investigate in this book. Your child is an intricate personality, not just a set of behaviors. Parenting is not merely behavior control, but is always a means toward the ultimate goal: helping your child to eventually assume responsibility for his or her own behavior. Because of this long-range goal of parenting, your reaction to specific behaviors will affect your child's self-concept, relationships, and eternal soul. This means that you, as the parent, need to anticipate, not merely react.

Parenting based primarily on response to specific behaviors usually fails to take into account the grandeur and potential of a child's total being, which is made in the image of God. In this book I hope you will feel the sacred responsibility parents have to cherish the past, present, and future of your child's life. Anything less than this shortchanges your child and can produce severe disruption in your home. I know you desire to do it right the first time. *Relational Parenting* will point you on the path to raising positive, strong kids in a troubled world.

Loving parents who anticipate and plan as they nurture their growing child will make a lifelong friend of that child. I'm sure that is what you want. Even if you find yourself in some deep water now, there is help. Read on.

Ross Campbell, M.D.
Chattanooga, Tennessee
July 1999

Chapter One

Two Approaches to Parenting

Like storm-driven waves in the darkest of nights, a society that has no light wanders around, searching for truth. Families, unborn babies, stability, peace, and the future are all at risk today.

—Joseph Stowell

Mary was such a wonderful child, so well behaved," her grieving mother, Beth, began, as she and her husband, Dan, talked with me in the counseling room. "She was such a joy and seldom gave us any trouble. Our friends said she was a perfect child. We tried to give her all the right experiences—church, music, sports. Dan even took karate with her for a while.

"She did have some conflict with her sister and brother occasionally," her mother continued, "but they are close now. Sometimes she seemed down and would keep to herself for periods of time, but we thought that was just her way. Most of the time she was content. And Mary has always had many friends.

"She was not disrespectful, although she did have a mind of her own. But she was certainly well disciplined—Dan saw to that. How could a child who was given everything, and who seemed so well disciplined, turn out this way? We never dreamed she would get involved in drugs. And we are so confused about the people she has been running with since she finished college.

To think we picked a Christian college to prevent this sort of thing! And now she wants to marry an illegal alien—the man we think got her pregnant. This is such a nightmare!"

"When did you first notice a change in Mary?" I asked.

"We first saw a change when we visited her at college during her junior year," said Dan. "She wasn't as eager to see us as we thought she would be, and yet we didn't think too much about it, since her grades were good and she seemed to have adjusted well to school. But when her grades began going down dramatically, and when she kept changing her major, we knew there was a serious problem. She finally graduated by taking a degree with the least requirements."

"Did Mary tell you how she spent her free time?"

"That was what bothered us the most. Even though she talked about various activities she was in, we never felt we really knew what was happening in her social and spiritual life. We thought she was involved in some Christian organizations on campus and was enjoying the typical life of a college student. We had no idea that she was using drugs or that she was involved with David.

"Where did we go wrong, Dr. Campbell? What can we do to help her now? We love her and want to be part of her life, but she is so cold to us. Not exactly hostile but distant. We can't believe she is the same girl we sent off to college a few years ago. What can we do?"

MARY'S STORY

When I contacted Mary and asked if she would talk with me, she refused at first. But a youth minister who had been close to her finally persuaded her to come. As she sat in my office, I saw her as an attractive twenty-two-year-old who appeared sad and somewhat unkempt in personal care. Obviously pregnant, she moved slowly, her face displayed little feeling, and she appeared withdrawn. After a few minutes of small talk about her college, her family, and friends, Mary began telling me a disheartening story.

"I don't know exactly where to start, Dr. Campbell. I love my parents and family and I had a good childhood. Nothing awful happened to me, as it did to so many of my friends. In fact, I don't really understand why I've made such a mess of things. I wanted to be a marine biologist, but just couldn't get it together. When I didn't make the grades I needed, I lost interest in everything. Even though I had great friends and opportunities at college, I just wasn't happy. My professors tried to help me in every way they could, but nothing helped."

"What about your social life before college and since then?" I asked.

"I dated some in high school—as much as I wanted to, I guess. I didn't have sex, if that's what you mean, but we did make out some. In college it was the same. I didn't go to bed with any-one until David. I met him while I was working as a waitress part-time, to earn a little money. He was working as a busboy—he doesn't have a green card yet. His family wants to come to the United States too, and David hopes to help them, but he has to get his own situation straightened out first."

"Mary, tell me more about David," I asked.

"Well, he is a wonderful person who really cares about me. He isn't very religious, but he's so compassionate. He cares about people and wants to help his family. He says he really loves me and is helping me fight this drug thing. I'm not doing too well in that area—I've been in treatment for six months now but can't seem to shake it. I do OK for a while and then slip back. Can you help me?"

Mary's story is not unusual. She is a sensitive, good-heart-ed, and well-meaning young woman who has difficulty thinking for herself. Because she is easily persuaded, she is led by stronger and more selfish people. Mary typifies a new pattern of maladjust-ment in our older children and young adults—a pattern seldom seen until recent years. Wonderful and seemingly normal children from fine families, whose parents tried to do their best, are em-broiled in heartbreaking crises by the time they are young adults. To those who knew her, Mary was not a candidate for serious or life-destroying problems. Nor are countless others who find them-selves in similar situations. How do these children and teens turn out this way? We think we can explain such problems when the young people come from backgrounds of poverty, abuse, or divorce, but not when they have been raised in loving and stable Christian families.

TWO APPROACHES TO PARENTING

Can we explain why more and more children are doing so poorly, including those from seemingly good homes? Yes, there are definite answers for why so many children and their parents are having such unprecedented troubles today. Those answers are not simple, and yet many of the problems arise from one simple, basic area of parenting: how we respond to our children's needs. Two phrases seem to encapsulate how parents deal with their children's needs. Some parents practice the *reactive approach to parenting*. Others follow a *proactive approach to parenting*. The key difference in the responses of the two kinds of parenting is this:

Reactive parenting responds primarily to what kids do.
Proactive parenting deals primarily with what kids need.

The reactive approach results in punishment-oriented parenting. The proactive approach anticipates and then seeks to meet the most basic needs of children. This positive, proactive approach is the more effective way to rear children.

THE KEY TO EFFECTIVE PARENTING

To consistently express love for the child is the basis of effective parenting. It doesn't matter that this expression varies greatly from one place and time to another. What does matter is that the parents meet the child's needs and that the child *feels* genuinely loved.

The basic needs of children do not change. Yes, the context, the externals, the expressions in society change—and the changes we have seen in the last few decades give parents real cause for concern and can complicate the delicate job of rearing our children. Often society seems to be uniting against what we are trying to accomplish in the home. Yet, in the midst of this, we must remember: The basic needs of children do not change. And the first of those needs is to feel loved.

Most parents love their children, but not all express their

love in ways that have meaning for the child or that meet the total needs of the child. If the surrounding culture or community is sufficiently similar to the family's values, parents can often get by with less than effective parenting, since someone else will take up the slack. But, when the culture is far divergent from what the parents believe and value, the burden rests much more heavily on them to meet the needs of their children. Today there is almost no room for error.

As a parent who wishes to raise responsible children of good character at the start of this new century, you know the largeness of the task in front of you. You cannot rely on most schools or neighbors or the community to give you significant help. Often you can't even trust your own relatives or your church to reinforce what you are teaching and modeling at home. And you certainly can't trust the media, with its messages.

We live in a society that is often blatantly anti-child. Consider what is happening:

- Children's needs are generally given low priority. Even hardened criminals receive better social services than many of our children.

- Many schools have become places of chaos instead of refuges where children can learn. The Centers for Disease Control in Atlanta have listed school violence as a public health concern in the United States.

- Advertisers exploit the weaknesses and desires of the young.

- Abortion practices make children not only optional but expendable. When adults don't want a child, they can remove the unborn from the womb to "protect the woman's needs" while ignoring the child's.

- Child abuse remains a blight on society in the early twenty-first century.[1]

All of this means that as parents you need more than ever to understand what your children need, both now and for the future, so that you can consistently work to meet those needs in the relatively few years you have your dear ones in your home.

WHICH "EXPERTS" CAN YOU BELIEVE?

In recent decades, parents have been deluged with advice about raising their children. This flood of materials is a fairly recent innovation, starting slowly in the seventies and accelerating greatly in the two decades following. Now child-rearing advice has become a whole industry, with publishers and organizations vying to see who can gain the most influence through their materials.

With so much advice, whom can you believe? Not all these "experts" agree on how to deal with children. Even in the rapidly rising religious publishing industry you will find some significant divergences in the approach to parenting. It is hard to know how to evaluate all that you hear and read, particularly if you are a conscientious parent wanting to do your best.

My own books have been part of that flood of resources, though they have been different from the majority. In 1976 I wrote my first book to parents, *How to Really Love Your Child,* because I needed something to give to parents of my young patients. That book and those that followed have been based on decades of clinical experience as a child psychiatrist and also on my experience as a dedicated father. They are based on research, on the experiences of many other caring mothers and fathers, and, yes, they are grounded in scriptural truths. The principles have been proven in countless homes and situations around the world.

After I wrote *How to Really Love Your Child,* my pastor, Ben Haden, introduced me to Victor Books, which then published the book for a wider market. I was amazed when it became a bestseller and was later translated into more than thirty languages and distributed in many countries.[2] My files are filled with thousands of letters from thankful parents who have applied its principles with their children.

When I wrote that first book, our own children were three, seven, and fifteen. Now they are grown and have established their own homes. So far they have presented Pat and me with one granddaughter, and we are hoping for more grandchildren. Every day we thank God for our children. They have become the kind of adults we hoped and prayed they would be.

Because my philosophy of rearing children has disagreed with that of some of the popular experts, I want to indicate my approach at the beginning of this book. I believe we see a clear choice in parenting advice. On the one hand, parents are urged to deal with their children mainly in response to specific behaviors. On the other hand, I and some other professionals urge parents to approach their sacred task by understanding the life needs of their children and then setting out to meet those needs. The first way I call "reacting to behaviors." This is reactive parenting, and it usually doesn't work very well. A better approach to parenting is based on "anticipating needs." This is proactive parenting. Effective, relational parenting is proactive.

FOUR FOUNDATION STONES OF EFFECTIVE PARENTING

I believe that your children's needs can be grouped in four areas, each key to effective parenting. I call these the foundation stones of effective parenting. In this book we will look at ways in which these needs are not being met in many cases, and then at ways that you as parents can work with your children to set these stones for their total good and happiness, both now and in the future.

Your consistent expression of love needs to take very specific forms that adapt to the age and developing personality of your child. That expression, which forms the basis of effective parenting, consists of four foundation stones:

- Meeting the emotional and nurturance needs of your child

- Giving loving training and discipline to your child

- Providing physical and emotional protection for your child

- Teaching and modeling anger management for your child

As you seek to meet children's needs while they are young —whether at age two or ten or twelve—you always have your eye on the goal. The ultimate goal in rearing children is to prepare them for responsible and happy and successful adult lives. This means that you anticipate for your children, since they cannot do this for themselves. If you merely react to specific behaviors and try to give your guidance only when unfortunate things have already happened, you will always feel frustrated in your parenting, since you can never catch up. This, in turn, will leave your children feeling frustrated with themselves and also with you, because their immature actions are doing the leading. They need for you to lead and anticipate and train, not merely react to their behavior.

If you provide what your children need in the above four areas, you will then be able to gradually release them with a fair degree of confidence that they are able to make good decisions that will take them into productive and happy adult living.

MARY AND THE FOUNDATION STONES

Let's take another look at Mary and her family, in terms of these four needs that all children have.

Emotional/Nurturing Needs

Adequate and appropriate emotional nurture is the first foundation stone of effective parenting. In order for children to have good self-esteem and be able to cope with the pressures and stress of life, they must first feel that their parents love and truly care about them. Yet many children and adults are having problems with anxiety, depression, and feelings of inferiority. These prevent them from functioning well in our difficult, competitive society, and so many of them take what seems the easy way out —destructive behaviors.

Mary revealed to me that she never felt that her parents deeply loved her. She knows in her mind that she was cared for while growing up, but she never has felt genuinely loved. Recognizing that feeling has been somewhat of a surprise to her, since she grew up in a nice home where her physical needs were generously provided for. In fact, she often feels confused and guilty for the poor relationship she has with her parents. Although she loves them, she has never been able to express this love. This inability makes her wonder if something is wrong with her. As a result, she tends to stay away from her parents, and is unable to communicate with them as she would like to.

In talking with Mary's parents, I became convinced that

they deeply loved her. But they had gotten the idea that they had to make sure their daughter was not "spoiled." This meant that their primary way of relating to her was with correction and punishment—or threat of punishment. If they could have been able to observe their behavior toward Mary, they might have understood why she didn't feel their love. They were focusing first on behavior and reacting with punishment, rather than focusing first on Mary's emotional needs. A child is much easier to discipline when she first feels loved.

If Mary's parents had looked after her deep needs of love and affection and kept her emotional tank full, she would have probably escaped the negative feeling about herself and about authority that so hinders her now.[3] She would have been stronger in setting her priorities and also in resisting the pressures around her. She could then have accomplished what she truly desired for herself, instead of being controlled by negative subconscious motivations such as rebellious anger and destructive behavior.

Although it is obvious to a trained observer that Mary was never given ample emotional nurture, this was far from clear to her. The confusion that this has caused her, together with the lack of emotional security she needs, has kept her from doing her best in school and relationships as a young adult. She needed to feel truly loved by her parents, and the lack of this has been a major reason for her great distress.

Training/Discipline Needs

Most parents are misled into using harmful training techniques. Those techniques continue to be recommended by well-meaning people who fail to see the entire picture. A reactive approach seems to work when children are young, so parents believe their children are doing well. But when the parents continue these reactive methods, the approach eventually undoes both the children and the family. Then, when their children drift away into bad lifestyles later, these parents are bewildered. In Mary's family, this was evidenced by an overemphasis on punishment.

Physical/Emotional Protection Needs

Every child needs a parent to protect him from physical

and emotional harm. It is surprising that the need for adequate protection must be emphasized to parents today, since there are so many negative influences in our society. Some of these unspeakable threats to our children are carried out in secrecy, as unscrupulous people make money by reaching our children behind the backs of parents.

We know there is a disconnect between what parents assume about their children and what the children are in fact doing. This becomes evident in the disparate results in surveys in which the young people admit their behaviors and the parents tell how they think their kids are behaving.

We thank God that there are still many wonderful, wholesome, uplifting, and inspiring influences remaining in our society, and we must fight to keep them. But we also need to be aware of the growing number of negative and hurtful influences that can touch our children.

Mary told me, for instance, that she was not protected from the unwholesome influences of the various forms of media and the Internet. Because she was not able to think for herself, and was easily led by strong peers, she was not ready for the temptations she met when she was no longer at home.

Although Mary was raised in a Christian home and was active in her church, she would have benefited from more protection from the evil influences of our society. Concerned parents need to work closely together to form ways to keep our children occupied with healthy activities, including those that are physically challenging. Otherwise, they may be tempted to engage in unwholesome and even destructive activities. We need the help of church staff, as well as teachers and community leaders who have similar values.

Good parents can feel as if they are involved in warfare, and they are. Our society contains too many sinister people who are actively engaged in using children to make money or satisfy other desires. Increasingly news media report on solicitation by child molesters on the Internet. Child pornography is big business. Our government has not been active in attacking those who threaten our children. As parents we must shoulder the major responsibility of providing a healthy environment. However, none of us needs to be alone in this. We can look at it as a great opportunity to work together as fellow Christians for the kingdom of God.

Teaching/Modeling Anger Management Needs

The most misunderstood area of training is in the handling of anger. In fact, I believe that the most difficult part of parenting is training children to handle their anger in a mature fashion. Few parents know how to manage well their own anger either, since most of them have never been trained to do so. And few parents are aware that it is their responsibility to train their own children in this area.

We have seen a serious escalation in public displays of anger in recent years, and we can no longer rely on most institutions in society to give much help in the training of our children. As parents, training our children to manage their anger is an essential task; yet most of us are unaware of what we should be doing.

Without parental training, we have a population that is handling anger in increasingly primitive and immature ways. We see the evidence of this everywhere—personal violence, resistance to legitimate authority, and hostile attitudes. In chapter 6 we will explore this critical subject.

Mary revealed that she experienced much anger in her home as she was growing up. Her parents argued a great deal and this kept the atmosphere tense and uncomfortable, especially for the children. Mary was quite fearful of parental anger, particularly from her father. This prevented her from talking openly with her parents and also made her highly resentful of them. She often felt a desire to hurt their feelings or upset them and make them angry. Her resentful attitude occasionally turned to defiance, although she seldom confronted her parents directly.

It was painful for Mary to tell me all of this, because she truly loves her parents, and she knows that they would be profoundly hurt if they heard her saying these things. But as a result of her parents' actions, Mary has had a great deal of trouble handling her anger, since she has never been trained to do it in a mature way. And, her parents have not been good role models for her and her siblings.

CHANGING OUR PARENTING APPROACH

If you're a parent reading this and think, *Well, I've made mistakes, and I don't know if it's too late or where to begin,* take heart. If your child still lives at home and you're willing to change some approaches, you can still play an effective role in shaping your child to reach that ultimate goal: readiness for adult life.

When I think of change, I think of Shanna and Mike, parents of one child, Jim. When Jim was fifteen, Shanna called me. "Jim is a good-natured boy, very conscientious," she explained, adding that he had been easy to control and discipline, especially in his younger years. "He used to get along well with other children and was involved in his church youth program. My husband and I didn't have any real concerns about Jim until he was twelve, when he became increasingly withdrawn. He talked to us and others much less. We assumed this to be typical preadolescent moodiness. However, his grades began slipping and he wanted to drop out of sports and the youth program. That's why I called you."

As we later met together, I discovered that Jim's parents were loving and committed Christians who felt a genuine concern for their son. What they didn't know was how depressed he had become, or that their approach to parenting was accentuating his problems. They had long assumed that strong discipline was the primary way to relate to their son. This meant that they were very reactive in their parenting. That is, Shanna and Mike had been reacting to Jim's behavior instead of focusing on how they could provide the nurture he needed. They had been greatly influenced by Christian parenting books that emphasized "discipline" without sufficiently providing the guidance necessary to adequately nurture a child.

Whenever Jim would make a mistake, misbehave, or displease his parents, they responded negatively. This usually included harsh and unpleasant verbal responses and often physical punishment. Naturally, anger was part of their reactions, although Shanna and Mike were not as aware of this as they should have been, nor of the tension this was producing in Jim. They really thought they were giving Jim the "right" kind of parenting, the kind advocated by so many "experts."

As we talked about their family dynamics, Shanna and Mike soon recognized that they needed to enlarge their understanding of the essential needs of children. Eventually they were able to change their focus from reacting to initiating, from responding to first giving and meeting Jim's emotional needs. As they did this over time, he began to come out of his depression.

Now, a year later, Shanna and Mike continue to put their parenting energies primarily into meeting Jim's basic needs. This has freed Jim to once again be his happy and productive self. This satisfying story has a wonderful ending because Shanna and Mike learned to parent in a fulfilling and giving way. They now anticipate Jim's needs, instead of reacting to his behavior.

LOOKING TO THE FUTURE

Whether our children are five or fifteen, we all think ahead to the day when they will be on their own. In one sense, all of our parenting activities are focused on that day, as we seek to prepare our children to eventually take responsibility for themselves and be able to function well in the adult world. Such preparation proceeds at a slow pace, one step at a time.

Today, that pace seems slower than ever, as older children are taking longer to become independent. This increase in time has its implications emotionally, physically, and financially. As parents we need to be aware of this recent phenomenon so that we are able to work with our children to handle it in a positive way. In a culture that is often threatening and confusing to our children, we must prepare them for the future.

Mary's parents had a difficult time releasing her in a healthy way because they were not providing for her needs in terms of the four cornerstones mentioned earlier in this chapter. However, as they discovered, it is never too late to make corrections and to seek divine help for the family. God is the Expert at making something wonderful out of a terrible situation.

NOTES

1. Portions adapted from Ross Campbell, *Kids in Danger* (Colorado Springs: Chariot Victor, 1995), 21–22.

2. Since then more than 1.4 million copies have been sold in the United States and abroad.

3. The concept of a child's emotional tank, or emotional needs, is discussed in detail in chapter 2. In addition, see Gary Chapman and Ross Campbell, *The Five Love Languages of Children* (Chicago: Northfield, 1997), 17–20.

Chapter Two

How Did We Get to Where We Are?

*W*hen *the foundations are being destroyed, what can the righteous do?*

—PSALM 11:3

A s I think back to my growing up years, I remember them as a simpler time for both children and their parents. We all knew what was expected of us, and we usually felt we could comply with this. The world was our oyster—it was predictable and friendly. World War II had ended, and people felt a great relief and also an enthusiasm for what was possible. Young couples began families that would fuel a baby boom from the midforties through the early sixties. Crime was low and most streets were safe. The only drug we had to worry about was alcohol. Most people had similar values—at least publicly. There was a common understanding of right and wrong.

THE GOLDEN FIFTIES

As we look back on our own history, it's always tempting to remember the greener grass and forget that every generation has its problems. And often those problems affect other social or racial groups more than they do our own families and friends.

That was true during the fifties, a "traditional family" time of larger families, a low divorce rate, and even lower inflation.

The period had its problems, of course. Americans saw a great deal of racism, sexism, and classism. Yet even with these inequities, the stability of the culture and permanence of nurturing families made it a predictable, safe, and friendly time in which to live.

In their book *The War Against Parents,* Sylvia Ann Hewlett, a white female, and Cornel West, a black male, took a look at those fifties. While they did not downplay the difficulties of the decade, they believe we must carefully consider the positive ingredients of that culture. West argued that the presence of intact, hardworking families and the network of family-supporting institutions, such as churches, gave him the stability he needed to thrive, even under segregation.[1]

Yes, I remember when cars had fins, when television did not control the time of most children, and when violence in children was essentially unheard of. Life was much more predictable. Teachers usually upheld parental values, and parents encouraged a healthy respect for teachers and other authority figures. Most young people finished high school and either went on to college or got a job. All men were eligible to serve in the military for six years, at least two of those in active duty. Employment was available to young people who were willing to work. In that postwar boom time, layoffs were rare. If life was not happy for everyone, at least it was stable. "Stressed out" and "burned out" were unknown phrases.

THE TURBULENT SIXTIES

During the early years of the Cold War, we Americans found a common enemy in the Soviet Union. We began the sixties united as a nation, one in our opposition to Soviet-style communism. Tensions boiled during the 1962 Cuban missile crisis, when Soviet Premier Nikita Krushchev was able to place medium-range ballistic missiles only ninety miles from American shores. As a young naval officer I realized that I could have been the one to give the order to open fire from our destroyer escort, as we turned back a Soviet freighter with nuclear missiles bound for Cuba.

The Russians and Premier Krushchev eventually backed down following a U.S. naval blockade, but the long struggle with the Soviet Union would continue. During this time, we were all together in defending ourselves against the "evil empire." Yes, we were Americans and magnificently proud of it. We had saved the world from Hitler and now we were saving it from the USSR.

And then, Vietnam and the youth counterculture came along. Violence and protests began on our college campuses, with takeovers of administration buildings, burnings of ROTC centers, and battles with police. Many young people condemned the military decisions being made in Washington, and their radical opinions that challenged institutions also extended to sex and drugs. The way of life we had taken for granted was under attack. Some missionaries I know were living in South America during the late sixties and received their news primarily from magazines, such as *Time* and *Newsweek*. Scheduled to return to the United States in 1970, they felt apprehensive about what they were coming back to, after years of pictures and reports of street riots and bombings and burnings. They wondered if the whole country was out of control.

A 1999 television documentary on the sixties drew viewers back into the turbulence of that time, showing its so-called sexual revolution and later legalization of abortion (in 1973), and the political intrigue that led to Watergate and a disillusioned public. Flower children gathered in San Francisco and later Woodstock to celebrate their newfound adolescent "freedom."

MANIPULATING BEHAVIOR AND THE SEVENTIES

While the youth revolution was being played out in the streets, something else was also going on during the sixties. A movement that was far more hidden was taking place primarily in university offices and laboratories. This was the popularization of a system of thought called *behaviorism,* the result of decades of experimentation with animal behavior. The application of this to children and young people was called *behavior modification.* Its beginnings in the sixties came to full flower in the seventies, as it exerted monumental influence on the rearing of American children, in both secular and religious families.

This system trains children to behave in the desired fashion by using *positive reinforcement* (injecting a positive commodity into a child's environment), *negative reinforcement* (withdrawing a positive commodity from a child's environment), and *punishment* (injecting a negative commodity into a child's environment). An example of positive reinforcement is to reward a child for appropriate behavior by giving him a piece of candy or fruit. Negative reinforcement might be to withdraw television privileges for inappropriate behavior. Punishment, sometimes called aversive technique, could be to pinch the child on the trapezius muscle—sending sharp pain into the upper shoulder—for inappropriate behavior.

Behavior modification, or B. Mod. as some liked to refer to it, became almost faddishly popular in the seventies, especially as educators demonstrated what their techniques could accomplish in the training of animals. I remember seeing a pigeon who had been trained to dance a Scottish jig. If animal behavior could become this predictable, just think of what could happen with children!

Behavior modification became the dominant school of thought in psychological training programs, gaining such wide acceptance that it became the primary psychological approach to child training and discipline. Its implications for child rearing, unfortunately, would be largely negative. B. Mod. focuses mainly on behavior and is totally unconcerned with the emotional needs of a child. It is a huge leap from laboratory rats to children, and these so-called "experts" forgot that children and rats are very different in their makeup. In the years following, behavior modification has become the principal system of child rearing in America, even if it is not labeled as such. When children are trained primarily with B. Mod., as most children inadvertently are, they can bear strong and lifelong effects. We see these in the attitudes of teenagers who have been so trained. When they are asked to do something, instead of responding in a productive and positive manner, they often convey, "What's in it for me?"

During the late sixties, when the youth of this country reacted to the Vietnam War as part of their countercultural revolution, many psychologists blamed "permissiveness" in the home as the cause. However, that was an incorrect assumption—child rearing had little to do with the movement. I agree with the late, great Christian philosopher Francis Schaeffer, who stated that the countercultural movement was due to the age, status, and maturity of our culture, and was precipitated by the Vietnam War, not by parents. The behavioral psychologists and well-meaning sociologists, however, argued that permissive parents had contributed to a counterculture that rejected established institutions. That argument was largely accepted, and this philosophy of discipline through behavior modification gained a larger following. That allowed B. Mod. to bloom fully in the seventies.

BEHAVIOR MODIFICATION TODAY

Failing to meet a child's emotional needs first and reacting merely to the child's behavior is the essence of behaviorism. A great problem today is that behaviorists have gained dominance in parenting philosophies, and this is especially evident in Christian circles. The result has been much confusion and conflict regarding the manner in which children should be raised. I recognize that behavior modification is occasionally effective and appropriate, yet never is it appropriate as the primary way of relating to a child.

Most behaviorists, including those who are Christians, do not honestly state that they are advocating behavior modification. The teachings of such people are very persuasive. Through their books and programs, these people have convinced concerned parents to use their behavioral methods—without ever saying that they are behaviorists, since this would not have been acceptable in many religious circles.

One behaviorist I respect is Dr. Ruth Peters, author of *Don't Be Afraid to Discipline.* She is one of the few honest behaviorists who admits her position in her book.[2] Dr. Peters speaks of love this way:

> Loving means being willing to take risks in order to help your children develop standards and behaviors both you and they are proud of. That's the essence of a good self-concept. Without the ability to choose right from wrong, your child's self-concept is in jeopardy. Loving means being willing to set limits that may anger or disappoint your child today so that he'll develop a high level of morality which will carry him into and through adulthood.[3]

Peters is correct in saying that feeling loved is critical for a good self-concept. And loving a child includes training. But before training will work, and for that child to develop at his best, he must first feel loved. Behaviorism contains little about loving a child—of keeping the emotional love tank full. I do recommend Peters's book for ideas and guidance on techniques in giving a child consequences of behavior, but not as a way to primarily relate to a child. When wise parents focus on a loving relationship with their child, that child will respond to behavior control. *The behaviorist focuses almost exclusively on the behavior and assumes that the child will feel loved simply because the parent is trying to correct his behavior.* That assumption is wrong.

I find ample examples of punishing a child and providing consequences of behavior in the behaviorists' writings, but almost nothing about transmitting love from a parent's heart to the heart of the child. Peters praises other books with messages similar to her own. For example, she describes *The New Dare to Discipline* by James Dobson as a "classic book." Tragically, many parenting books are behavioral but do not state that they are. As a result, Christian parents tend to assume that the books are thoroughly "Christian" in content, because they contain religious language and because the authors are Christians.

WHAT WENT WRONG?

When behavioral parenting books began to be published in the seventies, many dedicated and knowledgeable people in the area of family and children were shocked. They could not believe that trained professionals could advocate techniques that were so oblivious to the emotional needs and development of children. And they predicted that if parents, even very religious and concerned parents, adopted this thinly disguised B. Mod. system, the affected generation of children would begin to have emotional and behavioral problems that would contribute to the deterioration of society. They also predicted that the difficulties would become apparent in about fourteen years.

Tragically, these people were right. We have all witnessed the problems of young people from seemingly "good" homes. Their parents had high aspirations for these children and never expected the outcomes they have had to live with. Because they followed the advice of so-called "experts," they are confused about what went wrong.

What went wrong is that much of the Christian community accepted a philosophy of parenting based on behavior modification. This philosophy is the one we talked about in chapter 1, in which parents react to a child's behaviors rather than anticipate the child's needs. If a parent's main concern is to change a behavior, he will not think very much about the underlying needs of the child at age three or ten or fifteen. Millions of well-intentioned parents have followed a system of rewards and punishments without first meeting the emotional needs of their children.

In 1994, Josh McDowell and Bob Hostetler's book *Right from Wrong* documented what went wrong in so many homes. The book was based on a study directed by the Barna Research Group, called "1994 Churched Youth Survey." In the study, 3,700 young people in thirteen evangelical denominations were extensively and confidentially surveyed. The young people were intensely involved in church activities and identified their parents as loving and their family experience as positive. And yet the survey revealed that these teens were living on the moral edge, much closer to disaster than most people ever imagined. The results of the study revealed not only where the participants were behaviorally, but also where their younger siblings would be in a few years.

Large proportions of our youth—a majority of whom say they have made a personal commitment to Jesus Christ—are involved in inappropriate, immoral, even illegal behavior. The survey reveals that in the previous three months alone:

- Two out of every three (66 percent) of our kids aged eleven to eighteen admitted they had lied to a parent, teacher, or other adult.

- Six in ten (59 percent) had lied to their peers.

- Nearly half (45 percent) watched MTV at least once a week.

- One in three (36 percent) cheated on an exam.

- Nearly one in four (23 percent) smoked a cigarette or used another tobacco product.

- One in nine (12 percent) got drunk.

- Nearly one in ten (8 percent) used illegal, nonprescription drugs.

  The data show that young people from good Christian homes are succumbing to the pressures of our society. By the time they reach the age of eighteen, over half (55 percent) have engaged in fondling breasts, genitals, and/or sexual intercourse. Half (50 percent) of our youth say they're stressed out.[4]

When we compare this data with that of teenagers in the general population, we see that our churched young people do fare better than those who are unchurched. And yet, an overwhelming number of them are involved in lying, cheating, stealing, drugs, hurting people, and various forms of sexual activity.

Josh McDowell has said, "We may be one of the few societies in the world that finds itself incapable of passing on its moral teaching to young people." This is a matter of great concern, for if we do not pass the torch of faith and responsibility to our children, their lives will never be what we had hoped, and the impact on society will be severe.

WHAT IS THE ANSWER?

Parents must meet the emotional needs of their children if the children are to follow the example of their parents. And yet children cannot follow their parents in the journey of faith, belief, and moral integrity unless they personally identify with the parents. Nor can they identify with the parents unless the parents meet their emotional needs.

Parents who follow a reactive system to modify behavior will not meet the deep emotional needs of their child. The more behavior modification is incorporated into parenting, the more the parents are using reactive parenting. They are overemphasizing a child's behavior and using rewards and punishment based strictly on that behavior. Of course, your child's behavior is important; in fact, it is critical. But when parents emphasize behavior to the point of forgetting the child's emotional and spiritual needs, as well as needs for life training, they are almost insuring that the child will have severe problems in the years to come.

Reactive parenting results in an overuse of punishment, especially corporal punishment. Yes, there is certainly a place for punishment as we raise our children; but in the vast majority of homes, it is much overemphasized. Those experts who advocate behavior modification in child rearing, and in particular those who are Christian, seem to encourage spanking and pinching as the primary means of punishment. In some popular books, corporal punishment is advocated as the primary way to relate to a child.

When parents think of punishment, they should always consider what is the appropriate means for a particular child and the specific offense. There are occasions when spanking or pinching are absolutely destructive to a child. When parents keep the emotional needs and development of a child uppermost in their minds, they will be less concerned about modifying a particular behavior than they are in training the child in appropriate ways. Although this training certainly will include punishment at times, it will not automatically mean one form of punishment over another. We will discuss this more in later chapters.

MARY AND HER PARENTS

In chapter 1, I told you about Mary. When she was young, her parents were concerned that she would become spoiled. Dan and Jane loved Mary deeply and wanted to make sure that she did not become one of those children known for her misbehavior. And so they frequently used corporal punishment, to the point that they questioned whether they were resorting to it too often. At certain stages in Mary's childhood, she would be spanked several times a day, since her parents didn't know any other way to deal with her behavior. When Mary responded immediately to the spankings, Dan and Jane assumed that this form of punishment was "working." And when they talked with their Christian friends about matters of discipline, they were encouraged to continue using spankings freely, even if they felt somewhat guilty about it.

Unfortunately, Dan and Jane seldom sought other options

to help Mary learn to control her behavior, or even to question the reasons for her misbehavior. Also, they never came to understand their daughter or to find the most loving ways to train her. Because spanking and pinching were the primary ways they dealt with Mary's behavior, they didn't pursue avenues that would help them know her feelings or thoughts. Occasionally, they offered her rewards for making good grades and other pleasing behaviors. They regarded parenting as most parents do today—as a matter of controlling and training a child primarily with punishment. Consequently, they were unable to meet Mary's needs in a reasonable and logical way.

Because she was a compliant child, Mary presented no major problems to Dan and Jane—until she was older. When her resentments and anger finally came out, she displayed her anger in immature, self-destructive, and internally rebellious ways.

Dan and Jane are bright and caring people. If they had not been exposed to reactive parenting that emphasized behavior modification, couched in "Christian" language, they would have done much better with Mary. They would have figured out most of it on their own—at least well enough to prevent the catastrophic problems which now afflicted their daughter. And, if Jane and Dan had learned about the importance of emphasizing Mary's needs and discovering how to meet them, her life could have turned out beautifully.

REVISITING THE FOUR FOUNDATION STONES

Relational parenting is somewhat like foundation blocks at the corners of a house. It must have all four to be able to bear the weight of the life being built on them. Those foundation stones are the ones we talked about in chapter 1:

- Meeting the emotional and nurturance needs of your child

- Giving loving training and discipline to your child

- Providing physical and emotional protection for your child

- Teaching and modeling anger management for your child

If any of these is missing or is given the wrong emphasis, the parents will have difficulty with their children. In many good

homes, the final building block—the anger management stone—
is too small. And even though most parents deeply love their children, we find that parents have been unable to transmit love from
their hearts to the hearts of their children. The first building block
is usually too small. You can imagine how unstable a building
placed on this foundation will be.

When parents follow a form of child rearing that empha-
sizes behavior modification and reaction to specific behaviors, they
will not meet the emotional needs of their children. Therefore, the
children will not be trained in several areas, most particularly in
anger management. They will be prone to develop antiauthority attitudes that will lead to anti-parent attitudes and eventual rejection
of the parents' values and beliefs.

Such children will not have respect for legitimate authority
figures, teachers, and employers. And isn't this exactly what we are
facing today in our society? I wish with all my heart that parents
would take care of their children's emotional needs first. Then behavioral control would be so much easier. And best of all, our children would have healthy attitudes, toward themselves and toward
authority, and parents would find their relationships with their children much more satisfying. That's the power of relational parenting.

Reactive parenting that attempts to modify behaviors first
seems to work well when children are younger, and for this reason it has gained a wide following in parents who might be expected to know better. For instance, spanking brings instant
results in most children. And when well-known behaviorists recommend it, parents find it easy to overuse this form of discipline.
Yes, I acknowledge that spanking is effective—for a season—with
most children. But as children grow older and the spanking and
other negative punishments continue, their hearts fill with resentment and a determination to undermine their parents' authority
and wishes. Then caring parents, who thought they were doing
what was right for their children, feel totally confused and dismayed as their children fall into destructive behaviors and habits.
These parents, who have done their best, are also guilt-ridden,
blaming themselves for their children's grief and continually looking for the mistakes they made in raising their children.

Their primary mistake is that they followed the behaviorists into the punishment trap, something we will discuss more in chapter 3.

WHAT OUR CHILDREN NEED

In a 1995 report, the Carnegie Council on Adolescent Development identified "enduring human needs" that are essential for healthy development. Young people need to:

- have close and durable relationships with others;

- feel a sense of worth as a person;

- develop reliable bases for making informed choices;

- express constructive curiosity and exploratory behavior;

- find ways of being useful to others; and

- believe in a promising future.[5]

Meanwhile, the Search Institute of Minneapolis has analyzed four key assets that students need to develop in order to make wise choices:

- Sound values which provide a basis for making decisions and taking actions

- Social competencies

- Commitment to learning

- Positive identity

For our young people to be able to claim these key assets as their own will mean a commitment on the part of parents. But it also makes demands on the children and on the wider community.[6]

As parents, we all have a mental and emotional picture of what we want for our children, of the kind of people we want them to become. As we think about the many facets of their lives, we know in our hearts that we need to give them a dedication of all that we are as persons, to prepare them for life. This means reaching out to their emotions and their spirits, as well as to their minds and bodies. This also means that we approach this most important job in the world with the attitude that we are privileged to meet the needs of these dear ones—all of their needs. That means firmly fixing the four foundation stones: We will *(1) freely give our love, (2) train them to be able to live productively and with self-discipline, (3) provide physical and emotional protection, and (4) model and teach the best ways to manage anger.*

This is a noble calling. It must not be reduced to mere control of a child's behavior for the moment, so that we will not be troubled by inappropriate actions. This calling asks for our total involvement in the life of each child and of the family as a unit.

As we consider what we want for our children, we do well to look back to a little family in Bethlehem long years ago. The first Son of that family, Jesus, "grew in wisdom and [physical] stature, and in favor with God and men" (Luke 2:52). Such a brief statement, and yet so much love and training behind his favorable growth. What a wonderful example Mary and Joseph are of the kind of parents we want to be. The twenty-first century may be different from first-century Palestine, yet God's resources for us are the same as for Mary and Joseph. And the goal is the same: to rear children to wisdom, maturity, and love for God and men.

NOTES

1. Mary Stewart Van Leeuwen. "Parenting and Politics: Giving New Shape to 'Family Values,'" *Christian Century,* 29 July 1998, 719.
2. Ruth Peters, *Don't Be Afraid to Discipline* (New York: Golden Books, 1997), 71.
3. Ibid., 189.
4. Josh McDowell and Bob Hostetler, *Right from Wrong* (Dallas: Word, 1994), 8–9.
5. "Assets," Minneapolis: Search Institute, 1997, 2.
6. Ibid.

Chapter Three

The First Foundation Stone:

NURTURING LOVE

Dear children, let us not love with words or tongue but with actions and in truth.

1 JOHN 3:18

All parents know that their children need love, but few are giving those children the amount of proactive nurture and love that they need. To steadily develop in all areas of their lives, growing children need healthy and continuing relationships with adults who genuinely care about them and who regularly fill up their emotional tanks.

Few children feel truly loved and genuinely cared for by their parents, or anyone else. This is a major factor explaining why children are involved in personal crises during their adolescent years. And yet how can this be happening, when most parents feel that they deeply love their children? When most adults believe that caring for youth should be a top priority in our communities?

As in all human relationships, actions speak louder than words. Love and care for children need to be demonstrated, not only said or assumed. There are two reasons for this. First, we all tend to wonder if we can believe words that are not followed up by corresponding deeds. This is true for people of all ages, whether eight or thirty-eight years old, although adults are often able to understand that a love of some sort may exist, even if the messages are not consistent.

The second reason love must be demonstrated has to do with the needs of growing children. Our children come into this world with emotional and behavioral capabilities, but they have to learn verbal communication over many years. This means that we parents need to communicate love to our children primarily in emotional and behavioral ways. Of course, we should express our love verbally every day, while remembering that those verbal expressions will mean more to us as parents than they do to a young child. What makes the child feel loved is based much more on what we do than on what we say.

Having a warm feeling in our hearts for our children is not enough. And telling our children we love them is also insufficient. To transfer our love from our hearts to their hearts, we must love them on their terms, with active, clear displays of love. Such demonstrations of love carry far more weight with a child than verbal expressions. However, we should use both every day. For when our words and our actions combine in consistent ways to fill a child's love tank, that child then has the energy-producing nurture needed to grow strong in every way.

THE SETTING FOR EXPRESSING LOVE : THE HOME

How do we develop these consistent, ongoing expressions of love? The primary place where love is demonstrated to children is in the home.

"The most important relationship in the family is the marital relationship. Both the quality of the parent-child bond and the child's security are largely dependent on the quality of the marital bond. So you can see why it is important to help a husband and wife to have a good relationship before attempting to solve problems they may have in child rearing." I first wrote those sentences twenty-five years ago in my book *How to Really Love Your Child,* at a time when pressures on families seemed almost mild compared to today.

You will read a great deal in this book about unconditional

love. A healthy family home—one that nurtures children and meets their emotional needs—will convey unconditional love. Without an atmosphere of unconditional love, it becomes difficult for you to convey convincing expressions of your personal love to your child, since those expressions will be contradicting the very air your child breathes every day. While you may have some success, you still will be conveying mixed messages to your child.

A VITAL ELEMENT: UNCONDITIONAL LOVE

Real love is unconditional. The foundation of a genuinely meaningful relationship with a child is unconditional love, for only this will nurture a child emotionally and spiritually. Only unconditional love can ensure that a child will not be plagued with immature anger, resentment, guilt, depression, anxiety, and insecurity. For only unconditional love places the needs of the child first. Unconditional love is the vital element of the first foundation stone of proactive parenting.

In my thirty years of working with families, I have never found an exception to the following principle of child rearing: *It is impossible to correctly discipline children unless our primary relationship with them is one of unconditional love.* Today, many "experts" are trying to persuade parents to go against this truth. Some are urging parents to relate to children primarily with punishment. Others are trying to persuade them to use behavior modification—but almost never calling it what it is. Using punishment, such as spanking or pinching, or using B. Mod. as the primary way to relate to children, will result in disaster for both parent and children somewhere in the future. Both of these techniques focus only on behavior, without first taking care of the children's emotional and spiritual needs. Employing this reactive parenting approach to parenting can appear to yield some success for a while, but eventually both parents and children will have problems which could have been prevented if the children's needs had been met first.

Your child needs nurture. Without unconditional love, you will find it nearly impossible to understand your child's behavior or to deal with that behavior. Unconditional love is a guiding beacon for you as a parent. Without it, you are operating in the dark, lacking familiar and comforting landmarks. You can then easily lose your way and become confused, because you do not know how to deal with your child or with difficult situations.

Unconditional love will give you the landmarks to know where you are with your child and how you can best handle all situations, including discipline. Only with a foundation of unconditional love can you find the balance between being too harsh and too permissive or lenient. Only with unconditional love will you keep your child's respect. Only unconditional love enables you to meet your child's needs consistently and also prevents parenting from becoming a frustrating and confusing burden.

UNCONDITIONAL LOVE DEFINED

Unconditional love means loving a child no matter what. No matter what the child's abilities, assets, looks, or personality traits. No matter who the child may remind you of. No matter the history surrounding him. No matter what you expect of him. And, most difficult of all, no matter what his behavior happens to be— no matter how he acts. Of course, this doesn't mean that you always like his behavior. It means that you always love the child, even when you may detest the behavior.

Unconditional love is an ideal parents want to continually strive for. Only God can truly love unconditionally. Only He can always love us when we do not deserve to be loved. As parents we cannot fully achieve this, but we can love our children most of the time. The closer we come to the ideal, the better parents we will be.

When our children were young, I wish Pat and I could have said, "We love our children all the time, regardless of anything else, including their behavior." But, like all parents, we could not. And yet, we can give ourselves credit for having tried to attain the wonderful goal of loving them unconditionally.

You may find it helpful to remind yourself of the same things Pat and I often had to remember about our children:

1. They are children.
2. They will tend to act like children.
3. Much childish behavior is unpleasant.
4. If I do my part as a parent and love them, despite their

childish behavior, they will be able to mature and give up their childish ways.

5. If I love them only when they please me (conditional love) and convey my love to them only during those times, they will not feel genuinely loved. This, in turn, will make them feel insecure, damage their self-esteem, and actually *prevent* them from moving on to better self-control and mature behavior. Therefore, their behavior and its development is my responsibility as much as theirs.

6. If I love them unconditionally, they will feel good about themselves and be comfortable with themselves. They will then be able to control their anxiety and, in turn, their behavior, as they grow into adulthood.

7. If I love them only when they meet my requirements or expectations, they will feel incompetent. They will believe that it is fruitless to do their best because it is never enough. Insecurity and anxiety will plague them and be constant hindrances to their emotional and behavioral growth.

During those years as a struggling parent, for my sake and the sake of my sons and daughter, I prayed that my love for my children would be as unconditional as I could make it. The future of my children depended on this foundation. So does the future of your children.

AN INFANT'S SENSITIVITY

Children's emotions are exquisitely sensitive. From the very first encounter after birth, an infant can sense the mother's feelings. If the infant detects any hint of rejection from the mother, and later from others, she will be hampered in her development. This can affect her feeding and sleeping, and make her fretful and unhappy. If the mother is otherwise troubled, for example, ill or depressed, the infant can tell and retains this sensitivity for a season, and if that trouble continues indefinitely, even for a lifetime. Unfortunately, the infant has misinterpreted her parent's feelings as rejection, when actually something else is happening.

A child's first impressions of the world are through his feelings, long before he and his parents have any control over his behavior. It is the child's emotional state that determines how he sees or senses his world, his parents, his home, himself. This means that we must care for his emotional needs first—not only as an infant, but as long as we have the power to do so.

A foundation of unconditional love sets the stage for everything else that follows in a child's life. If she sees her world as hostile, rejecting, unloving, and uncaring, then anxiety, the great enemy, will become a profound problem, hampering her life in almost every respect. It will affect her ability to relate to others, to learn, to speak well, and to control her own behavior. Excessive anxiety makes a child vulnerable to all the negative influences in our culture. A major reason children and teenagers use drugs is to alleviate anxiety.

Reactive parenting doesn't consider this vital, underlying foundation of nurturance. Although some behaviorists admit that love is necessary to a child's well-being, I have yet to hear one of them explain how it can be provided other than through the use of rewards and punishment. By rewarding positive behavior and punishing negative behavior, behaviorism advocates a conditional love. And conditional love can never provide a child with what he truly needs—acceptance, love, and care based on the person. It focuses too intensely on behavior, without first giving the child what is necessary for him to be able to respond normally to correction. Without this love foundation, the child will eventually develop an attitude of resentment and rebellion toward the parent, although this may not manifest itself until adolescence.

YOUR CHILD'S EMOTIONAL TANK

The idea of an emotional tank is a figurative way of describing your child's emotional needs, which need to be met with your love, understanding, and kind discipline. The extent to which you keep this emotional tank filled has two crucial results in your child's life. First, it determines the emotional state of your child—whether he is anxious, content, angry, joyful, depressed, or happy. This concern is largely neglected in reactive parenting.

Second, the level of the emotional tank also affects your child's behavior. It greatly influences his response to training and discipline; it largely determines whether he is obedient, disobedient, whiny, perky, playful, or withdrawn. The better you keep the emotional tank full, the more positive your child's feelings and his behavior will be.

Here's an important truth in parenting that's crucial to nurturing your child: *Only when his emotional tank is full can your child be expected to be at his best or do his best.* Whose responsibility is it to keep that emotional tank full? Yours, as his parents. Your child's behavior is a good indicator of the status of his emotional tank. Of course, training and discipline are critical, but these are so much more difficult and often fruitless if the emotional tank is not kept full. Only as the emotional tank is kept full can a child be really happy, reach his potential, and respond appropriately to discipline and punishment when needed.

As we pray, "God, help us meet our children's needs as You do ours," we can have confidence that He will provide. In Philippians 4:19 we read, "And my God will meet all your needs according to his glorious riches in Christ Jesus."

Children do not have the ability to initiate love on their own. They basically reflect or give back the love which is given to them. If they do not receive love, they have none to return. If they are given unconditional love, they learn to reflect or return unconditional love. The source of such unconditional love and of the desire for it is God, and the sensitivity in filling our children's love tanks with such love—and with kind discipline and understanding —comes from God. (See also 1 John 4:19 and Proverbs 3:5–6.)

If they are given conditional love, they may never learn to return mature, unconditional love. They simply continue to love conditionally—the most immature way to relate to another person. In reactive parenting, which focuses on a child's behavior, there is little or no room for unconditional love. This explains why parents who fall into the trap of reactive parenting find themselves using punishment as the primary way of relating to their child. Under such circumstances, the child's emotional tank will not be filled.

RECALLING MARY

That was a major cause for the confusion felt by Mary, the young lady we met in chapter 1. The love between Mary and her parents was conditional. Dan and Jane expressed love toward their daughter when she did something that pleased them. Otherwise, they were generally critical of her performance, thinking that they were motivating her to do better. If she brought home a 90 on a paper, they asked why she hadn't scored 100. Although Dan and Jane loved Mary, they displayed their love in ineffective ways, based on her behavior.

As a result, Mary grew up feeling constant anxiety and confusion. She somehow knew that her parents loved her, but she never *felt* that love. She yearned for a close and warm relationship with her parents, but tragically she was never sure where she really stood with them, because she always felt their critical and conditional love. They thought that withholding their affection and warmth for the times when Mary excelled would make her do better. Mary, however, was an average child with average assets; she seldom excelled, so she seldom received genuine approval and affirmation as a person.

Like so many parents, Dan and Jane were afraid of "spoiling" their child. They followed the parenting books that advocated rewards and punishment based primarily on behavior. They also found themselves victims of the punishment trap. Unable to keep Mary's emotional tank filled, they failed to develop a warm, meaningful, and trusting relationship with her.

This behavioral approach seemed to work well when Mary was very young. But as she grew older, she came to feel that her parents were not concerned so much about her needs as they were about their own esteem as parents. By the time Mary was a teenager, the lack of unconditional love had taken its toll. Mary found herself resentful toward her parents and determined to undermine their authority by doing the opposite of what they wanted. Since she had been a compliant child, Dan and Jane were puzzled by this turn of events. Because Mary had never learned to love her parents unconditionally, she now behaved in a way that pleased them only when they did something that pleased her. And with

Dan and Jane acting the same way toward Mary, no one was conveying love to anyone, since they were all waiting for the other to do something pleasing.

What a mess! And yet we see this all the time as children reach adolescence and are still in the normal passive-aggressive stage—something we will talk about more in a later chapter. It reached the point that Dan and Jane were so bewildered and resentful that they finally decided they must seek help for their family. Their situation was sinking deeper and deeper into frustration and hopelessness. Some friends had encouraged them to get tough with Mary and demand respect and obedience. Others said that she simply had to pay the consequences for her bad behavior and learn from that.

It is never too late to turn a bad situation into one of healing as Mary's parents were eventually able to do. God is wonderfully kind and desires the healing of our families even more than we do. It always pays off to never give up on any problem, to love our children unconditionally, and to see them through the hard times. Although they may express this in an objectionable way, many children today have a justifiable sense that they are missing something essential to their personhood. What they are missing is unconditional love. They have been deprived of a full emotional tank and are lacking the very fuel they need to navigate successfully through the twists and turns of life.

HOW TO EXPRESS UNCONDITIONAL LOVE

Without unconditional love, our children are being deprived of a full emotional tank. They are lacking the fuel they need to navigate successfully through the twists and turns of life. While parents should not focus primarily on a child's behavior, they do need to use their own behavior to express love to that child, to keep the child's emotional tank full. Remember, children are behaviorally oriented; they understand your direct actions better than your words.

There are four primary behaviors parents can employ to give unconditional love to their children, and I want us to look at three of them in this chapter, as ways to put our love into action. We will consider the fourth, training, in the next chapter.

Eye Contact

Every child continually looks for his parents' love. When his emotional tank is low or on empty, he asks through his behavior, "Do you love me?" One way he asks is through his need for eye contact. He may say, "Mommy, look at me!" or "Daddy, look at me!" This is an expression of need. Your child wants your love and attention.

It is easy to give loving eye contact, and yet few parents do so because they are unaware of its importance. The more parents use loving eye contact with a child as a means of expressing love, the more that child is nourished and the fuller is his emotional tank.

When we talk with adults, we want them to look at us. We tend to favor people who are able to make continuous, pleasant eye contact as we talk with them. Some people are unable to do this because they were not given such eye contact by their parents when they were growing up. And they are usually unaware of their crippling handicap.

Mothers and fathers who follow reactive parenting may give loving eye contact only when the child performs well and brings pride to them. This kind of conditional love can have devastating effects. We must remember that eye contact is one of the primary sources of a child's emotional nurture. When parents use it in a primarily negative way, a child cannot help but see the parents in a negative way. When the child is small, she may be obedient and docile because of fear. But as she grows older and the feeling of being unloved continues, that fear often gives way to anger, resentment, and sometimes depression.

As I talked with Mary, it was clear that she had difficulty making continuous and pleasant eye contact. Because she was aware of this, she tried to correct the problem; however, when she was under stress, she could not do so.

One mistake many parents make—even, occasionally, those who practice proactive parenting—is to avoid or withdraw eye contact as a way to show disapproval or to punish. This is both a common and cruel form of punishment, and it does great damage to a child. *Eye contact should be used as a continuous way to give love.* Children learn how to live by watching their parents. If they receive consistent, unwavering eye contact, they will learn how to use eye contact in a healthy way also. But when their parents use eye contact in a way that shows annoyance, or to punish, the children can become social cripples, using eye contact in a way which is annoying to others.

This will hinder any child in making meaningful relationships and will put him in a situation of disadvantage in his adult life. Unless he can correct this behavior, he will tend to be more lonely and feel rejected by his peers. In fact, the best liked and most popular children are those who maintain pleasant eye contact with other people.[1]

We know that an infant's eyes begin to focus around two to four weeks of age. The first image which holds the child's attention is a human face, and especially the eyes. As the child gains eye coordination, she searches for another set of human eyes. At first these can be any eyes, but soon she is looking primarily for her mother's eyes. Her eyes are searching like radar antennae. When they find their target, another set of eyes, they lock on. At this tender age, she is already feeding emotionally, trying to fill her emotional tank.

And, even before the child can control her eyes, she is able to feed emotionally from her mother through eye contact, for her eyes are set to look into the mother's eyes during breast-feeding. In these earliest months, this little one is learning so much about the world. She is in a hurry—her basic personality, modes of thinking, style of speech, and other critical traits will be well fixed by the time she is five. Such a simple gift to offer a child—warm eye contact—and yet so crucial to future development.

Physical Contact

How loving is appropriate physical affection, yet few children receive adequate physical touching from their parents. Most parents touch their children only when they have to—when bathing or dressing them, putting them in the car, etc. Children will receive an occasional hug and kiss, but that's about it. Too few parents take advantage of their wonderful, almost effortless opportunity to keep a child's emotional tank full. When physical contact is used along with eye contact, so much the better for making the child feel loved.

In speaking of physical contact, I do not mean only hugging and kissing, two expressions that cannot be used on a continual basis. I am speaking of all types of physical contact—touching a child on his shoulder or the back of his arm, tousling his hair, scratching his back, gently poking him in the ribs, and on and on. All of these encounters tell the child you love him; they keep his emotional tank full. And if we do it whenever we have the opportunity, we will be showing unconditional love to our child.

A study from the University of Miami Medical School Touch Research Institute demonstrated that touch aids physical growth as well as mental well-being. As reported in a *Reader's Digest* article, the study found that premature babies who received three fifteen-minute periods of slow, firm massage strokes each day showed 47 percent greater weight gain than their ward mates not receiving this attention. The preemies who were massaged also exhibited improved sleep, alertness, and activity. Up to eight months later, they displayed greater mental and physical skills.[2]

You can include eye and physical contact in your everyday dealings with your children in a natural way. This type of affection—casual, frequent, and appropriate—is a precious gift to them. Along with focused attention (the third primary behavior), this is a most effective way to fill your children's emotional tanks and enable them to be their best.

Sadly, Mary did not receive this type of eye and physical contact from her parents. She never felt secure and was always looking for affection from others—the affection she should have received from her parents. This made her susceptible to the tragedies that befell her later.

Physical contact really pays off during the adolescent years. Parents who have shown great amounts of it earlier will find that these years are so much easier and more enjoyable. Teens who have been raised with an ample amount of physical contact will be comfortable with it. This will make it so much easier to keep their emotional tanks full, especially when they become uncommunicative. If they resist eye contact and focused attention, physical contact may become one of the few effective ways to keep their emotional tanks full and make sure they continue to feel loved.

A word about your children's responses during the teen years. Teenagers often have stages where they do not want to be with or talk to parents. Even then it remains critical for parents to keep their emotional tanks full. This is not easy when teenagers are in a withdrawn mood. However, at such times it is often possible to make physical contact with the child. When teenagers are in such a mood, they are usually so absorbed in themselves that they hardly notice a casual touch from parents. Your touches, therefore, should not be fewer. Instead, maintain or increase the number of touches.

Physical contact is a means at your disposal to offer unconditional love to your child. You can use it in so many ways, many more than I have suggested here.

Focused Attention

A third way to meet your children's need for nurturance is focused attention. This takes more effort on your part than eye and physical contact. In fact, it often takes sacrifice of time, something that you may feel is in short supply. It can also make demands on you when you least feel like giving it—when you are tired or unwell or pressured to finish your own work.

Focused attention means giving a child your full, undivided attention so that she feels she is truly loved. It is an attempt to make that child feel like the most important person in the world to you. It is making that child feel so valuable to her parents, in her own right, that she deserves your complete, undistracted attention and unreserved regard.

You might wonder if constant focused attention will somehow "spoil" your child. This is not the case. You spoil a child by failing to train her, not by loving her too much. In the Gospels, we see how Jesus felt about children.

> People were bringing little children to Jesus to have him touch them, but the disciples rebuked them. When Jesus saw this, he was indignant. He said to them, "Let the little children come to

me, and do not hinder them, for the kingdom of God belongs to such as these. . . ." And he took the children in his arms, put his hands on them and blessed them (Mark 10:13–16).

Clearly Jesus valued children and did not feel His time with them was a distraction from other tasks. Similarly, the Old Testament Scriptures ascribe great value to children. "Sons are a heritage from the Lord, children a reward from him" (Psalm 127:3). When Esau met his brother, Jacob, after many years apart, he asked, "Who are these with you?" And Jacob answered, "They are the children God has graciously given your servant" (Genesis 33:5).

If you want to be an exceptional parent, give your children ample focused attention. In doing so, you will be meeting the most demanding need your child has. Unfortunately, most parents have a hard time recognizing this need, much less fulfilling it. It is so easy to substitute favors and gifts for genuine focused attention. They take much less time and energy.

But in the long run, you will save yourself great amounts of time and energy and grief if you spend the needed time giving your children focused attention. Not only will they do their best, feel their best, and behave their best, but your relationship with them will be at its best. And in later years you will not have to undo the harm that comes from being neglectful of this need.

SETTING YOUR PRIORITIES

Our children require our time. Yet as parents we also function as homeowners, employees, and church and community members. We conclude we do not have enough time to carry out all of our obligations in the way we want to. And we don't. This means that something has to give. If we don't come to grips with this fact, we fall into what is called "The Tyranny of the Urgent": taking care of the urgent things of the moment while neglecting the important things. If we naively assume that everything will somehow get done and take care of the urgent things first, we will fail to care for what is really important. If the urgent rules life, we will not give focused attention to our children and probably not to anyone else either.

Because of the lack of time, we must determine our priorities, decide what we really want to accomplish, and then plan our time accordingly. This means that we need to control our time. Near the top of our priority list should be our children. They need our attention to develop as they should. If we come through for them, we will be rewarded many times over.

As a parent you need to decide what matters most to you. What priority does your child have in your life? If you don't determine this, your child will receive *low* priority and will suffer from the lack of attention. I have known fine people who succeed in most areas of life but fail miserably in giving their children a high priority. The children have multiple problems, though they come from fine homes and parents who are good people—good people who have not made their children a priority.

The object of focused attention, along with eye contact and physical touch, is to give your child the feeling, "I have my mommy or daddy all to myself." "I am the most important person in the world to my parents." To give a child this treasure is to be on the road to success in parenting.

A FORCE FOR GOOD

In our insecure world, our gifts of focused attention and unconditional love are among the greatest forces for good we can supply. Never before has it been so important to give our children self-confidence, self-reliance, and balance in their emotional and spiritual lives. Without this, they will suffer from anxiety and insecurity, and their emotional and psychological growth will be impaired.

As you consider how you will arrange your time priorities, remember, the best way to give a child focused attention is to spend time with her alone. When my children were young, I had a hard time arranging time for this, but I learned to make the effort. When my daughter was studying music, I arranged my schedule so that I could pick her up after the lesson and take her to a restaurant for supper. During these times together, I could give Carey my full attention and listen to whatever she wanted to share with me.

Being alone with your child in this way is so productive. Here you can develop that special, indelible relationship your child desperately needs to face the realities of life and to prepare for the future. A child will remember such moments years later, when life becomes more difficult, and his drives for independence create confusion and conflict. And when your child is grown, he will remember the times spent with you and be comforted and strengthened.

The stakes are especially high today, for what is worse than a wayward child, adolescent, or adult child? And what is more wonderful than a well-balanced and happy son or daughter?

This is your responsibility—and privilege. The key is to stay available to your children, to be there when they need you. During the teen years, children may need time to warm up with you so that they can share their innermost thoughts. It is a blessing to have developed a relationship with your older child in which he can and will share his feelings with you.

We have talked about the importance of spending time alone with each child. However, this is not always possible. Sometimes you can give the sense of being alone even when others are present. You do this by offering increased eye contact, by turning toward the child and staying in that position for some time. And, if possible, you can give some physical contact. You might even wink at the child or give some sign. My favorite signal was to place my index finger by the side of my nose and then move it toward the child. They would almost always return the signal and then give me a big smile.

Yes, giving focused attention is often time-consuming and can seem burdensome to already exhausted parents. But it is the most powerful means you have in keeping your children's emotional tanks full and investing in their future.

NOTES

1. A classic 1971 study by the Department of Child Psychiatry at the University of Florida College of Medicine found that children in a hospital pediatric ward were visited more frequently when they had regular eye contact. The less popular children, those whose rooms the nurses and volunteers entered less frequently, displayed less eye contact, typically looking at the visitor briefly, then immediately glancing down and away.

2. Lowell Ponte, "The Sense That Shapes Our Future," *Reader's Digest,* January 1992, 87.

Chapter Four

The Second Foundation Stone:
TRAINING
AND DISCIPLINE

We are not primarily put on this earth to see through one another, but to see one another through.

PETER DeVRIES

One morning when I finished a dental appointment, I was hungry and went to a nearby restaurant to have some lunch. As I was standing in line to order, a mother with two small children recognized me—I had been her doctor when she was a teenager. She came up to me, threw her arms around me, and said, "Dr. Campbell, do you remember me? Michelle Morgan. I'd love to talk with you."

It quickly became clear she didn't want a light social visit over lunch. She told me that she had some problems that were ruining her life. Fortunately, Michelle was with friends who were happy to care for her two children, so I agreed. We sat down to have our lunch together and to talk. Michelle began by telling me of her deep frustration in knowing how to discipline her children, ages three and eighteen months.

"I just don't know what I'm doing, Dr. Campbell. I feel so inadequate as a mother. Also, I remember the type of mothering I had, and I'm afraid that I'll raise my children the same way. My husband keeps telling me that I'm a great mom, but I can't believe him.

"I see the problems most of my friends are having with their kids and wonder how I will ever manage. I so much want my children to be happy and to grow into good people."

Michelle is like many parents today. There is no school for parents, and the changes in our fast-paced culture have made parenting very confusing. Most young parents simply raise children the way their own parents raised them, and they assume they know enough to do an adequate job. It is somewhat natural to feel this way when children are small, but when the children grow older, the parents realize that they do not have all the answers. They also recognize that they have made some mistakes they wish they could correct.

We don't have that luxury anymore. It is ever more important to do it right the first time. We don't have the same room for error as parents had in times past. This means that we need a clear understanding of the needs of children, and it is precisely in this area that so much skewed thinking has taken place.

TOO MUCH LOVE?

Many people believe in the "too much love" theory—that a child given too much love will be spoiled. They also believe that the cause of a child's problems is a lack of discipline, by which they mean punishment. Therefore, they withhold love and emphasize punishment. But as we have already noted, every child has a basic need for demonstrated love. So what happens? The parents get caught in the "punishment trap." They relate to the child primarily through punishment, and neglect the love they should be constantly demonstrating. Over time, mired in the punishment trap, the parents find that their influence as parents is damaged or destroyed. Worst of all, these parents fail to convey love from their hearts to the one they truly love—their child.

It is essential to first meet the emotional needs of our children. Then we can discipline and train with real effectiveness. Then, in turn, we can be confident; we can relax and truly enjoy our children. As caring parents, we have no right to punish our children without first carrying out our responsibilities, the primary of which is to meet their need for our love.

Most parents are quite confused at this point, thinking punishment comes first. If they follow this discipline-first method, they will have increasing difficulties with their children in the years to come. But if they follow the path of first meeting the children's emotional needs, they will find all aspects of parenting to be more effective and enjoyable.

WHO'S IN CONTROL HERE?

The Manipulative Child

Discipline implies the parents are in control. However, in more and more households, parents have lost control to their children. We see three- and four-year-olds who are running their parents ragged, with full knowledge of what they are doing. Three-year-old Josh, who wanted to go with his parents rather than stay with an aunt for the evening, staged a highly dramatic performance in which he threw himself on the floor and shrieked repeatedly. It almost worked, except that the aunt urged the parents to go on their way. She assured them that Josh would be fine, as soon as they were gone. After they left, she asked him, "What was that all about? Were you trying to run your parents?" Exhausted as he was by his efforts, he just nodded yes.

Never underestimate the power of a child to behave in a manipulative manner. He will try to twist you around his little finger. She will try to become a powerful little tyrant. If this is not brought under control while the child is young, the behaviors will become more pronounced over time. In households where one or more children are in control, the parents feel increasingly confused and the child's domination becomes even worse. While the parents are spreading their focus in many directions and perhaps are feeling increased financial and career pressures, the child may be exerting focused attention in one direction—getting and maintaining control.

The contest for power and control is exacerbated by the growing tensions many parents feel when they are stretched too thin, trying to keep everything together. When they are exhausted, they lack the energy and patience to deal with their children in a positive way.

These parents are often too tired to contribute what they should to their marriage. Recent findings have shown that the combined pressures of life have dramatic effects on the marital relationship. Sexual problems have increased dramatically in our society. And when both spouses work, they often arrive home tired and not ready to contribute. All of this tends to make parents react harshly to the bad behavior of children, instead of dealing with it in a calmer way.

As the atmosphere of the home becomes more tense, the level of confusion between parents and children rises, and so the vicious cycle continues. The contest for power and control continues. These parents have got to return to first things first and regain control of their lives and their home.

Tommy: "*I'm* in Charge"

Jeff and Margie complained that they were at a loss as to how to handle their son, Tommy. When he wanted something, he would immediately begin crying, without asking for what he wanted. Before they even knew what he wanted, Tommy was screaming with a piercing tone that could put a banshee to shame.

Finally, Tommy was kind enough to yell at Jeff and Margie, telling them exactly what he wanted. "I want that toy!" "Ice cream, ice cream. Now!" By this time, they were frantically trying to give him whatever he wanted, just to get him to stop screaming. If this weren't so heartbreaking and unpleasant, it would be hilarious. In this home it was far from funny, for the parents became so frustrated that other times they would be screaming at Tommy. "Tommy, that's enough! Shut up and you'll get your toy." Now the entire household was out of control, and it was a draw as to who was acting in a more immature manner. That parenting is an adult occupation was not obvious in this home.

When Jeff and Margie had friends or family over, Tommy really assumed control. He knew that his parents would do almost anything to keep him from humiliating them, and so he had them at his mercy. Naturally, his behavior caused the visitors to feel nearly as embarrassed as Jeff and Margie did, and also to wonder why these seemingly normal parents couldn't control their child.

They would think, and sometimes say, "Why don't they just spank him?"

Jeff and Margie were wise enough to seek help earlier rather than later. They knew there must be an answer that was eluding them, and they decided to find it. Because Tommy was four and not fourteen, they were able to make some major corrections. The first of these was for them to learn to meet his emotional needs first. Then they had to learn how to train him in appropriate behaviors and to apply loving punishment when that was called for.

Because his parents took their parental responsibilities seriously, Tommy now is a happy and relaxed young teenager. He and his parents get along well, partly because his parents have learned to remain calm and pleasant but firmly in control. They learned the hard way that parents must retain control at all times. Being firm does not mean being inflexible. It does mean that parents will maintain their composure while they try to figure out just what is happening and how they can best deal with it.

Being in control also means that parents must not relate to their children out of fear. Today we see many parents polarized on two extremes, both of which are disastrous. Some are overcontrolling, harsh, and punishment-oriented, while others are too permissive and afraid to establish controls for their children. These two extremes have the same basic cause—fear. Both kinds of parents fear the dangers present in this culture for their children. The first group fears that if they don't control the situation, the children will become deviant. The other group fears that if they anger their children, the children will rebel against them in dangerous ways. Raising children in such an atmosphere of fear is unhealthy for both parents and children and will inevitably lead to trouble. These parents need to learn how to give loving discipline to their children.

WHAT IS DISCIPLINE?

It is essential to understand that discipline is not synonymous with punishment. Yes, punishment is a type of discipline, but the most negative type. And punishment should be only a small part of discipline. The main reason parenting has become so difficult, and that many children are doing so poorly, is that the parent/child relationship has become primarily negative.

Parents have it in their power to make that relationship positive. It only makes sense to use all the positive resources available first before resorting to the negative ones. Yes, there are times when punishment is definitely appropriate, but most parents are using punishment as the primary means to discipline their children. This is reactive parenting, and it is in large measure responsible for the antiauthority attitude we see in so many children.

It is important to correctly understand what discipline is. *The most important part of good discipline is for parents to make a child feel loved.* Then parents can proceed to the other part of good discipline: *to train that child in mind and character to enable him to become a self-controlled and constructive member of society.* Discipline involves training, and effective discipline uses every type of communication available: guidance by example, role-modeling, verbal instruction, written requests, teaching, and providing learning and play experiences. As you can see, all these items are positive.

Yes, punishment is one part of discipline and definitely has a place in training a child, but we should never use punishment as the principal means. Guiding a child toward what is right is far superior to punishing a child for wrong action. Discipline means training, and parents are responsible to first love the child and then provide for all aspects of training necessary over many years. When the child feels loved, when the emotional tank is full, the child is in the best mode to receive the training.

A child must identify with the parents in order to accept their guidance without resentment, hostility, and obstructiveness. When the child fails to identify with the parents and doesn't feel loved, she considers each parental request as an imposition and learns to resent it. Many children today have a negative orientation toward parental authority. This eventually extends to all authority and results in their doing the exact opposite of what is expected. Such disrespectful behavior extends beyond the home to the school and other public places, like shopping malls.

How do you train your children to be respectful of other

people and of proper authority? By rearing them in such a way that they will remain emotionally attached to you in love and respect. Again, this requires that you (1) love them with unconditional love, (2) keep their emotional tanks full, and then (3) give them the proper training that they need for life.

HOW A CHILD LOVES

Before you can effectively discipline your child, you need to understand the way a child loves—which is quite different from the way a mature adult loves. Because children are immature, they love in an immature manner.

Consider first an adult example. Henry loves Barbara deeply and wants to marry her. He is doing his best to be loving to her, kind, pleasant, considerate, and helpful. He is trying to earn her love. This rational approach to obtaining love is called *reciprocating love.* Henry is doing all that he can to secure Barbara's love in return. While adults should seek to love each other in an unconditional way, for the most part we are able to love only in a reciprocating manner. Only occasionally do we move to the higher level of unconditional love.

A child, however, is not able to love on either of these levels —unconditional or reciprocating. Being immature, a child loves in a self-oriented way. He loves by instinct, and through instinct he knows of his own need to feel loved. He is aware that he must obtain that love from his parents. However, he is not aware that his parents also have emotional tanks that need to be filled with unconditional love. His only concern is to feel loved himself.

When his love tank is full, he is not compelled to behave in such a way to get the parents to refill it with unconditional love. However, if it is low, watch out, for then he is compelled to frantically ask, "Do you still love me?" by his behavior. Remember, children are behaviorally oriented. How the parents answer the love question determines how that child is going to develop. It also determines how he handles his behavior. *The main cause of misbehavior is an empty emotional tank.* Of course, there are other causes for bad behavior, but the empty emotional tank is the most common. Also, an empty emotional tank will make misbehavior from other causes more severe and more frequent.

Why is it so important for parents to understand how a child loves? Most parents believe that a child should try to earn their love and affection with good behavior. And yet, the child is simply too immature to do this. A child naturally tests parental love by his behavior, especially when his emotional tank is low. If parents do not understand how he loves, they will be confused and totally exasperated when the child does not act as they expect. They will misunderstand his normal behavior as unloving and disrespectful.

Many times a child misbehaves because she is pleading, "Do you love me?" When her parents assure her that she is indeed loved, they are taking the pressure off her; she need not continue to test their love with more misbehavior. However, if the parents fail to understand and think that she should earn their love with good behavior, they will continually be frustrated. They will regard her as disrespectful, ill-behaved, and unloving, when all the time she was simply asking in a childlike way, "Do you love me, Mommy?" "Do you love me, Daddy?"

"WHAT DOES MY CHILD NEED?"

When a child misbehaves, there is always a need to be met. We need to ask, "What does my child need?" Unfortunately, most parents ask themselves the question, "How can I correct my child's behavior?" This question almost automatically leads to punishment, regardless of what is occurring at the moment. When parents resort to punishment first, they cannot later easily consider the real needs of the child.

When you ask yourself, "What does my child need?" you can proceed logically and decide on a proper course. The need may be met by punishment, but not usually. If you overlook the need behind the misbehavior, you will not be able to do the right thing for your child.

When your child misbehaves and you ask yourself, "What does my child need?" the next question should be, "Does this child need her love tank filled?" It is important that you go about this rationally and logically. It is so much easier to train a child if she feels genuinely loved.

Of course, a child's misbehavior should not be condoned.

But you should deal with it rightly—neither too permissively nor too harshly. And you should make sure that you have taken care of her love needs first. Occasionally, all that is needed in the midst of misbehavior is to fill the emotional love tank. Usually more is involved, but sometimes it really is that simple.

I remember one such occasion in our home when Dale was five and David nine. I had been away at a conference and was eager to tell my wife, Pat, all about what had happened. When she and the boys met me at the airport, I began to tell her about the various events and virtually ignored the boys on the ride home. Every time Dale said, "Daddy," I kept on talking to Pat. He tolerated this well at first, but by the time we were home, he was out of sorts, crying, whining, and being generally disruptive. He even had David upset.

What was my first impulse? I wanted to change his cranky behavior, and I soon asked myself that old natural question, *What can I do to correct this child's behavior?* My dear wife sensed my frustration and quickly whispered, "Why don't you practice what you preach?" Of course. I asked myself the right question, "What does this child need?" The answer stared me in the face. I knew that Dale's emotional tank was empty because of the way I had treated him. I had been out of town and on my return had given him no focused attention. He was asking me, as only a child could (by misbehavior), the old question, "Do you love me?" Actually, he was asking, "Do you still love me after being gone so long and acting as though it didn't affect me?"

Suddenly his behavior made sense. He desperately needed his daddy. If I had done anything other than give him what he needed, *me,* his behavior would have become worse. A raised voice, a direct threat, banishment to his bedroom—none of that would have worked. I am so thankful that I didn't goof on that one. I took Dale to our bedroom, held him close, and said nothing. That normally active little fellow was so still and quiet against me. He just sat there absorbing the nurturing he needed. Gradually, as his emotional tank was filled, he came to life and began talking in his confident and happy way. After a short conversation about my trip, he jumped down and ran off to find his brother. When I walked into the family room, they were playing together.

I wish all misbehavior stemmed simply from a child having an empty emotional tank. How much simpler parenting would be! But unfortunately, this is not the case. When you ask yourself, "What does this child need?" and have determined that the love tank is not empty, you then need to ask, "Is this a physical problem?" The second most common cause of misbehavior is a physical problem.

The younger the child, the more behavior is adversely affected by physical needs. You need to ask, "Is my child in pain? Is my child ill? Tired? Hungry or thirsty?" While the misbehavior shouldn't be dismissed, the problem can almost always be quickly relieved if it is caused by something physical.

FIVE WAYS TO CONTROL BEHAVIOR

However, many times bad behavior is not caused by an empty love tank or by a physical problem. In any home, some behavior problems are going to lead to a need for further limits and, at times, punishment. When a child is out of control, being defiant, or challenging parental authority, you need to use appropriate means of control. You have five ways to control a child. Two of them are positive, and you want to use them whenever possible. Two are negative, and you will need to use them occasionally. One is neutral and should be employed with care.

The effectiveness of any of these will depend on how well you are keeping your child's emotional tank full. They are (1) requests (positive), (2) commands (negative), (3) gentle physical manipulation (positive), (4) punishment (negative), and (5) behavior modification (neutral).

Requests and Commands

Making *requests* is a positive way to control a child's behavior. It is the best way to develop a loving relationship. Requests are pleasantly soothing to the child, and this is especially important when parents are controlling the child's behavior. Requests tend to be in a higher tone of voice and the inflection at the end of the sentence goes upward, as any question does.

When you use requests, you are also sending many nonverbal messages to your child. With requests, you are saying to your child, "I respect the fact that you have an opinion about this." You may also be saying, "I know that you have feelings about this and I respect your feelings." And, best of all, you are conveying without actually saying, "I expect you to take responsibility for your own behavior." Your child can become a responsible person when you give him the opportunity.

A child raised primarily with requests is enjoying the benefits of proactive parenting. He can come to feel that he is in partnership with his parents in the molding of his character. This kind of child rearing is not permissiveness. The parents are not giving up authority or respect. In fact, the child will have much greater respect for his parents because he will feel that they are not simply telling him what to do, but are interested primarily in what is best for him.

When requests fail, you need to issue *commands.* Because commands are a negative way to control behavior, they should not be used unless requests fail. Commands can provoke anger and resentment in a child. The parent issuing a command usually uses a lower tone of voice and the inflection at the end of the sentence is downward. This aggravates any irritation.

In addition, the nonverbal messages to the child are negative. Because you are telling a child what to do, with no choices or opportunity for feedback or discussion, you are conveying that the child's feelings and opinions about this matter are not important to you. Most of all, you are taking all the responsibility on yourself. The more you use authoritative techniques such as commands, scolding, nagging, or screaming, the less effective you become. But, if you normally use pleasant requests, then the occasional use of commands will generally be effective.

As a parent you have much power and authority, but not an unlimited amount. If you use your position of authority unpleasantly, you will have little left to control your child's behavior. This is particularly true as your child grows older. Today we are seeing more and more parents using up their authority and becoming helpless, even when their children are small. Since you don't have infinite amounts of authority, you don't want to waste it by being always negative and then having little left for the truly difficult or critical times.

Being pleasant but firm not only conserves your authority but enhances it, because you are gaining your children's respect and love, as well as their gratitude. You need to remember that their greatest fear is your anger and unpleasantness. When you use requests and stay positive as you are training them, their love and gratitude will put you in great stead with them for the rest of your life. They will never forget your kindness and love, and will always be thankful that you are their parents, especially when they observe other parents who are unpleasant and angry with their children. This is a key part of positive, relational parenting.

Gentle Physical Manipulation

Gentle physical manipulation is the other positive way to control a child's behavior. It is especially effective with young children, but can work well with older ones too. I like gentle physical manipulation because it can be used for behaviors that are not necessarily wrong but are not to your preference. Also, it allows you to continue to be positive.

Physical manipulation works so well with two- and three-year-olds who are in that normal stage of development that seems to require that they say no to any request. For instance, you ask, "Will you please come here to Mommy?" And your child answers, "No." If you resort to a command and say, "Come to me now!" she may again answer, "No." At this point you might be tempted to punish her, but that would be a serious mistake. Instead, *you can take care of this absolutely normal situation by gently bringing her to you.*

You are being positive, loving, and gentle with her. Your child knows exactly what is going on. She knows that you could have been "mean" to her, but you chose to be kind and loving. This is what builds a genuinely loving relationship between parent and child.

If your young child resists coming to you when you use gentle manipulation, you then know that you are dealing with defiance. Particularly with a toddler, it is not always easy to tell the difference between normal toddler negativism and defiance, and for this reason it is better at first to assume the behavior is negativism. Then if it turns out to be defiance, you have not done anything hurtful, and can go on to correct the defiance.

Punishment

Punishment is the fourth way of handling a child's behavior. It is the most negative and also the most difficult to administer. There are four reasons for this. First, the punishment must fit the crime, since children are so concerned about everything being fair. They know when parents are being too lenient in choice of punishment; they then feel that they are getting away with something. They know when parents are too harsh; they resent any inconsistencies in punishment between them and their siblings.

Second, appropriate punishment for one child may mean nothing to another. We saw this played out with our two boys. For Dale, the worst punishment was being sent to his room. He needed to be with the rest of the family. But for David, time alone in his room was an opportunity to play with his toys and read his books.

Third, the punishment used at any particular time usually depends on how the parents are feeling at the moment. If they are having a wonderful day, they will most likely be too lenient when punishment is called for. However, on a bad day, they will tend toward being too strict.

And, finally, the parent must be able to choose punishment appropriate to the age level and development of the child. What may seem fair for a seven-year-old may be totally wrong for a five-year-old. What may be right for a bright child may feel oppressive to a child of more average development.

Yet, as difficult as it may be for you to decide when and how punishment should be used, the fact is that you must be prepared to use it and to use it appropriately. You can help yourself in this by planning ahead, so that you avoid the punishment trap. This means sitting down with a spouse or good friend to decide on the right punishments for various offenses. You should do this for each child in your family, when you are calm and can think about the good of that child. Doing this will help you keep your anger in check when a child misbehaves.

When a child does something wrong, you need to quickly ask yourself the questions I suggested about basic physical needs and development: "Is my child hungry or thirsty? Is he in pain or not feeling well? Is he expressing the typical negativism of a two-

or three-year-old?" If you come up with a no to each of these, you should ask one more question: "Is this child being defiant?" Defiance is openly resisting and challenging parental authority—something that cannot be permitted. You must remain in control at all times, and this means that the behavior needs to be corrected. However, this does not necessarily mean that punishment is indicated. You want to break the defiance but do it with the least expenditure of your limited resource of authority. If you automatically use your most powerful and negative means of controlling your child's behavior, namely punishment, you are needlessly overusing your power at a time when you may not need to.

I have seen so many terrible situations in which otherwise wonderful parents have made this profound mistake. They have overused their parental authority on minor and normal conflict in the home to such an extent that they have little authority left for the really important problems, such as their need to say no when a child desperately wants to attend an unwholesome party.

Yes, you need to break the defiance, but you also need to use your head. Many times, a simple request will break the defiant attitude, especially if the child feels unconditionally loved. Or a command may be adequate, or gentle physical manipulation. When you follow a more moderate path, your child will know that you have chosen the kindest way to handle him.

And you will know that you have chosen the way of meekness. This is one of the most misunderstood concepts of Scripture, yet it remains one of the most mature ways to respond. Meekness does not mean you are passive and weak. Rather, it is strength under control. Meekness is having the power at your disposal but refusing to use it until absolutely necessary.

Jesus was the perfect example of meekness. He had infinite power and used it sparingly and only when absolutely appropriate. He held it in reserve and was selective in its use. He employed His power only when He was caring for others, not to ventilate His displeasure.

You need to do the same in your parenting. As your children see your wisdom acted out before them, they will learn this wisdom for themselves.

Spanking as a Punishment

Yes, spanking is one kind of punishment, and a highly controversial kind that needs a section by itself. No type of punishment is perfect, and spanking certainly has its positive and negative aspects. On the positive side, spanking usually has instantaneous results. This is especially true when a child is young. Also, spanking is convenient, since it requires no planning and no thinking. It can be used in an instant.

On the negative side, it loses its effect as a child grows older. And the more often it is used, the less effective it is. If overused, spanking creates resentment, anger, and anti-parent attitudes. Even by the best of parents, spanking can easily be done in an uncontrolled way, especially when the parent is quite upset or feeling poorly. It may then be considered abuse, a topic of national debate and concern. Opponents of corporal punishment argue that spanking condones and even induces violence in the child. This argument cannot be ignored when we consider the increasing violence in our society among children.

Another disadvantage of spanking is that it can leave deep and lasting emotional scars on a child. The physical pain of a hand, belt, board, or other instrument can last days, but the emotional feelings of fear, resentment, or even rejection can last much longer. I recently spoke with an eighty-seven-year-old man who said he was still tortured by the spankings he endured as a child. In this case, I think *beatings* might be a more appropriate word. Such painful memories from childhood are not uncommon.

Yet there are people who seem to remember childhood spankings almost with fondness. These are generally the people who advocate spanking. I believe these folks were the ones well loved by their parents. Because their emotional tanks were full, they could accept spankings from their loving parents as an extension of their love. And they recognize that the punishment helped to shape them into respectful, mature adults. However, this response to spankings is quite rare today. It is far more common today for children to feel unloved by their parents. In such a milieu, corporal punishment simply makes the parent-child relationship even more negative.

To depend on corporal punishment as the principal method of discipline is to make the critical error of assuming that discipline equals punishment. *Discipline is training the child in the way he should go. The better disciplined a child is, the less punishment he will need.*

There are people today who defend what they call a biblical approach to discipline by relying on three verses from the book of Proverbs: 13:24, 23:13, and 29:15. They seem to believe that corporal punishment is the primary way of disciplining and relating to a child. These folks neglect to mention the hundreds of Scripture verses dealing with love, compassion, sensitivity, nurturing, understanding, forgiveness, guidance, kindness, affection, and giving—as though a child had little or no right to these expressions of Christian love.

Proponents of corporal punishment seem to have forgotten that the shepherd's rod and staff referred to in Scripture were used almost exclusively for guiding the sheep, not beating them. A shepherd would gently steer the sheep, especially the lambs, by simply holding the rod to block them from going in the wrong direction and by gently nudging and prodding them in the right direction. The shepherd's rod was also used to rescue wayward lambs. If the rod was an instrument principally to beat a lamb—or a child—we all would have a difficult time with the words of Psalm 23, "Thy rod and thy staff they comfort me" (verse 4 KJV).

However, the meek use of corporal punishment, as a last resort, can prove useful. The best example I can give is something that happened recently to my daughter, Carey. She was working in the front yard as her three-year-old daughter, Cami, played nearby. Up to this point, Carey had found positive ways to discipline and train Cami without resorting to corporal punishment. But on this afternoon, Cami began running toward and in the street. "Cami, would you please stay out of the street? I don't want you to get hurt," Carey said. But a minute later, Cami had run back into the street. "Cami, come back here! Stay out of the street," her mother warned, and the little girl returned. But a third time she wandered into the street.

This time her mother went out into the street after her. "I told you to stay out of the street," Carey said firmly. "Now, I mean it." She placed both hands on Cami's shoulders and led her back into the front yard. Cami played in the yard a little more. But when she went into the street one more time, Carey felt the situation was serious enough that spanking was indicated.

For the first time in her life, Cami received a rear-end message. That message had quite an effect. When Cami's father drove into the driveway about an hour later, she ran to him and exclaimed, "Daddy, don't run into the street!"

Notice that her mother withheld the use of punishment until more positive forms of discipline were tried. In order, she used a request, a command, and gentle physical manipulation before turning to corporal punishment. The real issue here is not about spanking. It is about the emotional health of the child. I have seen many children who have done beautifully—with or without spanking. The more important issues are how well the child is loved and how well the child is trained.

As long as corporal punishment is used as a last resort, and with the parent not venting personal anger, it is possible to employ spanking without hurting the child. However, in my experience, once a parent learns to use the more positive and reinforcing ways to train a child, spanking is seldom needed.

Behavior Modification

Behavior modification is the fifth means to control a child's behavior. It uses positive reinforcement (placing a positive element into a child's environment), negative reinforcement (withdrawing a positive element from the child's environment), and punishment (placing a negative element in the child's environment). In a sense, B. Mod. is neutral, as it includes both positive and negative elements. However, this "neutral" form of training presents distinct, significant problems as a primary way of relating to a child.

The two primary problems in using B. Mod. as the primary method of discipline are: (1) It can prevent a parent from loving a child unconditionally, and (2) it may nurture a selfish orientation in the child—"What's in it for me?"

B. Mod. should be used sparingly. If parents overuse behavior modification, their child will not feel loved. The first reason for this is that the very foundation of behavior modification is conditional—the child receives a reward only if she behaves a certain way. Second, behavior modification does not deal with a child's emotional needs and cannot convey unconditional love.

B. Mod. has another danger: Its overuse will teach children to use the same method on their parents and other authority figures. They will do what the parents wish, simply to get what they want. This leads to manipulation.

But having given all these cautions, there are still times when behavior modification can be extremely helpful. One of these is when parents are having severe behavior problems caused by sibling rivalry. A second is for specific and recurring behavioral problems for which a child shows no remorse. Another is when an early teen girl has communicational conflict with her mother. The more the mother tries to deal verbally with the child, the worse the conflict gets. This is a normal stage that many girls go through at this age, and B. Mod. can work well. My favorite book on this topic is *Don't Be Afraid to Discipline* (Golden Books), by Ruth Peters. She is an honest author, admitting that she is a behaviorist. She uses behavioral techniques appropriate for specific problems. Her writing is excellent and should be read by every parent for a better understanding of this form of behavior control.

WHEN YOUR CHILD IS TRULY SORRY

There are times when you know that your child is genuinely sorry for his bad behavior and this is cause for rejoicing. It means that your child's conscience is alive and well. Conscience is a commodity in short supply in our society.

What is the raw material from which a sound conscience is created? Guilt. And what will wipe away the guilt, as clean as a new slate? Yes, punishment! Especially corporal punishment. And here is where parents so easily fall into the punishment trap. Incorrectly given or administered at the wrong time, punishment is destructive to a child and also to the parents.

You certainly do not want your child to be guilt-ridden, and yet, there is something infinitely worse—too little guilt. If you punish your child when he is already genuinely sorry, you are not only losing a rare opportunity to teach him one of life's greatest gifts, forgiveness, but you are directly interfering with his ability to develop a normal conscience.

What should you do when your child feels genuinely sorry for her behavior? I don't mean when she says, "I'm sorry. I'm sorry" just to evade punishment, but when she is truly contrite. What does your heavenly Father do when you are sincerely sorry for wrongdoing and ask His forgiveness? He forgives you and cleanses you from all unrighteousness. Shouldn't you do the same for your child?

When you forgive your children when they are sincerely sorry, you are teaching them to forgive. By your example of forgiving, you are training them to forgive. This so important, because there are many people in our society who cannot forgive others, and who are doomed to become resentful, bitter, and unhappy.

When you forgive your children, you are also teaching them to forgive themselves. This is a beautiful gift. You know people who seem unable to forgive themselves, and you don't want that for your children.

A child who is truly remorseful for a wrong done feels overwhelming love for the parent. This offers us the opportunity to grow even closer to this child whom we love so dearly. As parents we always must remember that our first responsibility is to meet the emotional needs of our children. And their most important emotional need is for love. Only after meeting that need can we find success in handling their behavior. Training in behavioral and anger management becomes much easier in children who feel well loved.

Chapter *Five*

The Third Foundation Stone:
PROTECTION FROM HARMFUL INFLUENCES

At some point between Lamaze and the PTA, it becomes clear that one of your main jobs as a parent is to counter the culture.

ELLEN GOODMAN

Like concentric circles spreading outward when a stone is thrown into the water, so your child's contact with the world outside of home widens each year, and more people and influences touch his life. By the time he starts school, you are well aware that you can no longer control all the people and ideas that come his way. And as he approaches the teen years, you may have good reason to be downright fearful about all that he is encountering, even in settings that are supposed to be safe.

In a society growing ever more permissive, it is our responsibility and privilege to train our children how to think rationally. We can prepare them to withstand bad influences and to recognize true and wholesome messages. We can even use messages from the cultures we abhor to train our children to recognize and resist them. In chapter 4, our emphasis was on training children to behave. However, behavior needs to be linked to right thinking, or the behavior at some point will fall down. For this reason, we are now going to look at ways to teach our children how to think well so that they can not only survive but thrive.

As our society continues to lose its spiritual and moral heritage, caring parents cannot leave the ethical and cognitive education of our children to other people. We cannot count on a consensus of values that we once took for granted in the schools, churches, and other institutions. I am not suggesting that we have no positive influences left. But I am saying that there is an alarming confusion today about basic right and wrong, in all segments of society.

Morality and values in our once-trusted institutions *have* shifted. This has made parenting all the more difficult. But it also provides more opportunity to help our children thrive and excel in the world they will face. It takes courage to choose the right way in a society where job candidates fluff up resumes with false credentials, citizens underreport earnings to the tax man, and students find clever ways to cheat on tests. The more our children become courageously ethical and clear-thinking persons of integrity, the more meaning they will have in their lives. Also, they will be able to exert a positive influence on society. Yet, the converse is also true: The less they have of integrity and right thinking, the more they will be influenced by elements and people just waiting to devour young hearts and minds. This has always been true, but never in such a pronounced way as it is today.

A YOUNG MAN'S TEST IN ETHICS

When my older son, David, was still in college, he served as a business intern for a hospital chain where he confronted this lack of values head-on. One day the supervisor told him to act as a consultant to a competing hospital chain, even though he was only an MBA student doing a research paper. He was told to spy on the competitors while he was in their corporate offices.

David was shocked and disgusted at this assignment and refused to do it. Later, during a visit home, we talked about it. "Dad, I'm sadly finding that this is the way things are done out there," he said. "I guess this was my first test in business ethics. I hope I can keep myself from caving in to that kind of pressure in the future. But I know it is going to be hard working in an environment like that." Now that he has been out in the working world for many years, I'm glad to be able to say that he has maintained his integrity.

Stories like this are not confined to the secular world. Some years ago an executive of a religious advertising agency sent a few of his employees to do some work for a Christian organization the agency represented. He told one woman that while she was in the client's office, she was to nose around and see what she could find—in other words, spy—to discover who else this group was doing business with. The woman refused to do what her boss asked, and she paid the consequences, as he withheld her profit-sharing for several years.

Of course, when your teenager enters the working world, even on a part-time schedule during school, you will not be there anymore to determine her response. This is why it is crucial that you teach your child now to think rationally and critically.

ELEMENTS OF RIGHT THINKING

To help your children mature as you desire, it is necessary to help them think rationally. They need to develop the ability to evaluate and judge for themselves by the time they are adolescents. And by the time they are seventeen, you need to feel confident that they have the background and training and judgment to be able to make most or all of their own decisions. This is necessary for their safety—and also for your peace of mind.

As you train your children, you are seeking to give them correct perspectives about the world and the way they fit into it. You are shaping their ideas of reality and enabling them to possess for themselves a strong and healthy value system. You are enabling them to become people of integrity. Only with this will your children be able to stand up against opposing values and unwholesome influences. Only with this will they be able to influence others toward what is good and wholesome.

Today many in our society feel it is just too restrictive to say there is a right way of thinking and feeling. As increasing numbers of adults hold this opinion, one result is that many parents are not passing on basic truths and values to the next generation. Convenience and the desire to make more money have taken the place of doing what is right and working for the good of others. Our society is increasingly unable to tell right from wrong. And yet integrity is the part of basic character which determines a person's ability to be honest, sincere, and trustworthy.

The three basic ingredients of integrity are:

1. Telling the truth
2. Keeping one's promises
3. Taking responsibility for one's behavior

Not long ago most people in our society honored integrity in each of its elements. However, all three of these ingredients now are disappearing from society's standards of righteousness. Let's review the loss of belief in these three elements of integrity—a loss we must combat as we rear our children to have right values.

Telling the Truth

Truth-telling is based on more than societal order. It is founded in the notion that there is some objective truth on which we base the truths of our lives and our communities. It is not difficult to see how President Bill Clinton developed his values that led to accusations of lying to a grand jury. He did not have the early training he needed to walk with integrity and truth. The president had power, ability, and a brilliant mind (he was a Rhodes scholar). Yet even such a brilliant person can reap untold destruction if he does not have the feelings and values necessary to think rationally.

Clinton's behavior leading up to the impeachment findings was neither rational nor logical—something he admitted. However, he never admitted that he lied. Those in Congress who insisted that telling the truth is essential were often made objects of ridicule, told they were interfering with the smooth working of government and threatening the country's stability and the people's elected choice.

Lying affects *all* of our personal lives. It is perhaps in the home that it does the greatest damage. Lying to one another in the family not only causes dismay for those who are being lied to and frustration for those who are lying; it also distorts relationships in the home and may eventually destroy them. And those who are lied to consistently do not forget. Their trust has been broken and they may always view the liar with suspicion. This is particularly harmful to children whose parents have lied to them. As they mature, they may never know whom to trust.

Keeping One's Promises

Another area of integrity being eroded is keeping one's promises. Our promises include casual agreements that have little long-term consequence and extend to formal promises, such as business contracts and sacred promises, such as marriage vows.

One such contract that is increasingly being challenged is infant adoption. Much of the complication in adoption today happens because birth mothers make legal promises and then pull back and sue the adoptive parents. While the court battle drags on, the child may continue for some years in the only home he has known, with his adoptive parents. In one case that has nearly bankrupted the adoptive parents, a church organization intensely interested in family records is backing the birth mother and also paying all her legal costs. The issue of the birth mother's feelings should be considered; yet the church does not seem to strongly consider the importance of the integrity of the promise made in writing by the young woman.

The question of personal integrity touches people in the area of financial promises that are so easy to make and not so easy to keep. The rash of repossessions and foreclosures and unmanageable debt affects all of us, as costs go up. I am not suggesting that all these people have dishonest motives, but in many instances they have demonstrated bad judgment. They seem unable to decide what matters most and then put their time and money there. Or, they believe that they will never have emergencies or unforeseen expenses. Or, perhaps they want so much to be part of some organization or lifestyle that they lose the sense they should have.

Even the best of us at times are tempted to fudge on promises or renege on agreements, and then blame someone else. If we have been well trained in the elements of integrity and are convinced of their importance, we can withstand the tempta-

tion. But without that training and conviction, we have little defense. We see this kind of weakness even in highly educated people.

In my home state, Tennessee, I know a psychologist—we'll
call him Bob—who signed a contract with a counseling center
which guaranteed him certain benefits. In return, he agreed that
should he decide to leave, he would not compete with that center
(by having a practice nearby) for eighteen months. Because the
center provided for each staff psychologist to a maximum extent,
if any one of them broke this agreement, everyone else would be
jeopardized. Nevertheless, Bob soon went to work for a competing organization. This created such a crisis in the first counseling
center that it was forced to take Bob to court.

Although Tennessee law upholds such contractual agreements, the judge for some reason ruled in Bob's favor. Not only
had Bob, a highly educated professional, challenged the contract
he signed, but a judge with a law degree overruled the promise.
Both had disregarded formal written promises. The center went
under financially and has never recovered.

Taking Responsibility

A third area of integrity under attack is personal responsibility for one's actions. Many people today consider it foolish to
take responsibility for their actions if they can pin it on someone
else. We have become a nation filled with victims. In a litigious
country, we at times wonder if someone will tomorrow blame us
for their own actions. We regularly hear of the most frivolous law-
suits.

I remember well the only time I was ever sued as a physician. I had been assigned to a ninety-six-year-old woman who
was admitted to the hospital in a confused state of mind. She did
not know who she was or where she was, and she continually
tried to harm herself. We placed her in the special care section of
the hospital where she was under constant supervision and safe
from harm.

While there, she suffered a spontaneous fracture of the left
hip in the same place she had had a fracture twenty years earlier.
"Spontaneous" meant that the fracture had no external cause but
happened because of weakness in the hip.

The family brought a lawsuit against me and the hospital for alleged negligence that resulted in the fracture. Fortunately, this case went before a judge who understood the absurdity of the accusations and dismissed them.

Taking responsibility for one's behavior is becoming so rare that it produces wonder and joy when we do observe it. This is especially true when we see it in a teenager or young person. Blaming others is now so routine that we expect it from our leaders. We even feel genuinely surprised when a person refuses to use this immature and primitive means of copping out.

TEACHING YOUR VALUES TO YOUR CHILDREN

In order to teach your children, you need to examine your own thought processes and feelings. Do you want your children to process life the way you do? Are you even sure you know how you come to your conclusions or how you make decisions? You do have some process by which you do these, and you need to share this with your children at various stages in their development. There is more than one way to make decisions and come to conclusions, and your children may eventually do it in a slightly different fashion than you do. That is all right, as long as they are holding close the elements of integrity.

Explain Your Thinking to Your Children

Unfortunately, most parents do not share their thought processes with their children. They just share their conclusions and opinions. But these do not help children know how and why their parents came to those conclusions and opinions. In fact, if parents persist in simply telling their children their opinions and conclusions, without showing how they arrived at those conclusions, they have good reason to expect that their children will someday reject their ideas, beliefs, and values. *It is essential to teach children how to think.*

One way to share your thought processes with your children is to follow up with the word *because* after you have shared a conclusion or opinion. This will remind you to explain why you feel and think as you do. It will force you to examine whether you are being rational and logical and will motivate you to be reasonable. When you are sharing your thought processes with your children, you are also sharing your feelings with them.

Few parents share their deep feelings with their children, and this is a serious mistake. Naturally, you don't want to share inappropriate feelings with them, but they need to know the majority of your feelings. Otherwise, the primary feelings you display to them are negative ones such as anger, displeasure, discouragement, disgust, and pain. If they don't know about those deeply held feelings you seldom talk about, they will be programmed to reject the feelings they do hear from you. It is important to often talk about positive and meaningful feelings and values with your children.

Recognize and Evaluate Your Own Past Feelings

Rational thought is based on feelings and beliefs. The congressional investigation of President Clinton during the impeachment proceedings demonstrated how people on both sides can vehemently believe that they are being logical when they come to opposite conclusions. How can this be—decent people on both sides of the issue thinking in such completely different ways, and yet both being logical?

We can be tempted to say that it is all political, but that is only part of the answer. Even if people are influenced by personal advancement or gain, we have to ask how they believe they are justified in their stand, when they are in such opposition to others considering the same matter. The answer is that our reasoning is most influenced by what we have previously believed and felt.

We use these past feelings and beliefs to legitimize and "prove" our conclusions. These feelings and beliefs are derived primarily from our parents and other persons from our childhood. This means that our backgrounds largely determine where we will stand on certain issues.

In our present society, great numbers of children are being negatively influenced by their parents. Because these parents are not being proactive in their training and discipline, but rather reactive, they are almost guaranteeing that their children will feel and believe quite the opposite from what the parents think they have taught them.

Some parents are creating great amounts of stress in their children by their irrational beliefs and behaviors. Some are based on fears, others on misinformation. Consider some of the strange religious beliefs abroad in our society, even among some Christian parents. Some parents blame the devil for things they don't like or are sure that their misbehaving children are demon-possessed. This creates unbearable stress in the children. More and more, we are seeing parents bring their children to counseling centers with problems such as learning disorders, tic disorders, and eating disorders—problems that are caused or aggravated by stress. Yet some of these parents say in the children's presence that they are demon-possessed and then they demand an exorcism. It is hard to describe what such craziness does to the children.

Wise parents will make sure that their spiritual beliefs are rational, accurate, and that they make sense and are healthy for their children. They will also help their children understand their spiritual values in belief and in practice. Such training should happen in a relaxed and positive manner. If parents try to train a child only when they are reacting to bad behavior, they will find it very difficult to engage in rational conversation about values or to share deeply held feelings.

One goal of training is to extend our moral and spiritual values to the next generation—to our children and beyond them to their children. This must be based on our innermost feelings and beliefs, not on reactions to a current behavior. When we express an opinion, we need to explain to our children why we think that way, on what we base our conclusions. And we need to do this in a calm and believable manner. Children cannot tolerate anger in their parents. In fact, this is their greatest fear.

TAKE TIME TO TALK

It is crucial that you regularly make time to talk with your children, from a young age. As parents, you are their primary teachers about life. When you talk with your children and, in the process, teach them the elements of clear thinking, you get ahead of the game in training. This is especially so in the management of anger, the most difficult part of parenting. When you show them the way by openly sharing your thoughts, feelings and values, your children are then free to do the same.

I am so proud of the way my daughter, Carey, and son-in-law are teaching their daughter, Cami, to express her thoughts, feelings, and beliefs verbally. When she is upset about something, Cami is able to say exactly what is troubling her and why. This makes it easy for her parents to understand her and then to ask the critical "Why?" when they need to know the reasons behind her confusing thoughts or behavior.

For some reason, many parents do not train their children in the most important lessons of life. Nor do most of them know when and how to allow their children to freely express thoughts and feelings. But when parents don't know what their children think and feel, they have nothing to work with in teaching rational thinking. Because of this, most children are unable to think logically for their age, never develop this ability and, even worse, never learn to manage their anger.

This type of training takes much time, but the rewards are tremendous. I regularly talk with parents who are in the dilemma of deciding whether to spend more hours working outside the home or spending more time taking care of the needs of their children. While some of these people are in financial situations that give them little choice but to work, many do have a choice. They should remember that the more time they spend with their children, training them in these crucial ways, the more money they will save in the future. Many of the problems parents face with older children are extraordinarily expensive.

THOUGHTS OR FEELINGS?

Our children need to respect their own feelings in order to respect the feelings of others. But first, we need to respect the feelings of our children before they can respect ours. We effect this by sharing our own feelings with them and then asking them to share theirs with us.

We need to remember that thinking and feeling are not synonymous. Most people base their opinions and conclusions on their feelings, without realizing that they are doing so. Instead of thinking logically, they simply react emotionally. They have never been taught to think. When they are confronted with the illogical basis of their conclusions, they again react emotionally and often with anger.

Express Feelings with "I" Messages

One way to express your feelings is to use "I" messages. In these, you use the personal pronoun in expressing your feelings about a matter. This prevents you from sounding unpleasant or hostile. You might say, "It makes me feel sad to see the councilman took money to vote for a city contract. That's taking a bribe." This way, you are expressing your opinions, remaining pleasant, and then giving the reasons you think the way you do. As your children talk with you about issues, over the course of many years, they will learn to express their own thoughts and feelings in appropriate ways.

Unfortunately, many people assume that their opinions are derived from logical thought, when they are actually their raw feelings with little refinement. Raw feelings are not reasonable. When children grow up in this sort of atmosphere, they have nothing to protect them from the unwholesome influences in the world.

When parents hear a child make a statement that is irrational, they can be assured that he is simply expressing his feelings. They may be tempted to argue with him, especially if he is a teenager. This is a great mistake, because it frustrates him and makes him more determined to hold to his irrational case. It is wiser to listen calmly to what he is saying and then tell him the parts of his statements that you can agree with or support. This helps a child be able to control his feelings and further discuss the matter.

Show Patience When You Disagree

Don't feel that you have to win in disagreements with your child right then and there. Learning to think well takes a long time and is part of the overall maturational process. As your child discovers that he can express his thoughts and feelings with you without your becoming disagreeable, he will be increasingly willing to share them. Even more important, he will become open to see issues from your point of view and to be taught and influenced by you. Once you and your child get into this way of handling disagreements, you will both find it more pleasant.

As you train him to think well, your relationship with him deepens. This is especially crucial when you are handling conflict with your child. He then trusts you to control yourself, and to be an example to him in handling frustration during disagreement and conflict. This will make the long and challenging process of parenting easier and more pleasant.

When you seek to train your child spiritually, you follow this same process of sharing your own thoughts and feelings and values. As his understanding of spiritual things increases, you begin to see its influence on the way he thinks and acts. It will become a defense to him. The young person lacking in values, and especially in spiritual values, is susceptible to all sorts of doctrines.

Another reason it is important for children to understand their feelings is that we live in a time when depression and anxiety are with us in unprecedented proportions. Many young people cannot handle the pressures and problems of life because they are so susceptible to depression and anxiety. This is one primary cause of the increasing and overwhelming drug problem. Young people resort to these artificial and dangerous means to calm their anxieties.

THE MISSING LINK

"Parents are the missing link in improving American education," according to Secretary of Education Richard Riley.[1] Although parents can assist the schools in many ways, their primary contribution is in nurturing their children's emotional needs. A child's emotional maturity is the most important requirement for his ability to learn and do well educationally.

It's evident in school today that many parents are not providing proper nurture emotionally or teaching their children to think clearly. Ask those who have taught for many years, especially in urban areas, and great numbers of them will tell you that they are dealing with children who are immature emotionally and whose habits are unstructured. Such children are not ready to learn.

One early elementary school teacher told us a bizarre story of a mother who angrily threatened her child's teacher because the teacher wanted the boy to eat Jell-O with a fork or spoon rather than with his fingers. The teacher, trying to reach an understanding, asked the boy how his mother preferred that he eat. "She doesn't care. We never eat together." Then the irate mother added, "My child has the right to eat his Jell-O any way he wants to."

This mother is teaching her son that he doesn't need to think. He can just act on his feelings—or rather, on hers. Also, she is teaching him disrespect for rightful authority. And she is making life more difficult for those who spend every day with her son.

If you want your children to learn well, be sure that they are at their age level of maturity emotionally and that they know how to think logically. You are their prime teacher for these most essential lessons in life.

ANTICIPATE WITH YOUR CHILD

His mother once told young Jeff that they would go to the zoo the next day. In reality, they would be going to the hospital where he would have his tonsils removed. She didn't know quite how to prepare him, so she did not tell him their true destination. After the surgery was over and Jeff awoke from the anesthetic, he screamed for hours. The child in the room with Jeff had been prepared by his parents for what would happen. Although he had a sore throat, he still enjoyed the ice cream that the nurses kept bringing him. He kept wondering why the other boy was having such a tough time.

Preparing Your Child

That kind of tough time is all too common. To make sure that our children have an advantage in coping with life, we need to help them deal with problems before they happen. We need to be careful how we do this, so that we don't try to prepare an eight-year-old for something she won't face until she is fourteen. But, prepare them we must, for this is one of the primary protections against what they will encounter in the near future.

How do we let our children know of potential dangers

without frightening them or producing anxiety? In a conversational manner we need to mention some of the things, both good and bad, that they may encounter. Think again about Jeff. His mother could have driven him to the hospital a day or two days earlier to show him the hospital and explain what would be happening in each location. Such preparation would have given Jeff confidence and let him know when he could look forward to seeing his parents after the surgery.

Anticipating a potential problem with a child is a way of making it happen, in part, before the event. The child has experienced the situation in his imagination and has already decided how to cope with the various eventualities. This means that he can be in control when the situation happens in actuality.

Preparing for Dating and Sexuality

A classic example of this relates to dating, especially for girls. A wise father will have "dates" with his daughter, taking her to dinner and various entertainments, to acquaint her with how it feels to be out in this way. Then, when she later goes out with boys, she will not feel anxious or confused about herself. Instead, she will feel in control and not be subject to another's wishes or control. That wise father will have explained to her how to handle difficult situations: She will know what to do and how to get in touch with her parents if trouble arises.

She will have a good sense of security and confidence. The daughter will know and perhaps tell herself, *I've been out before, with Daddy. I can think for myself here and can handle this situation without having to follow anyone else's direction. If I need help, he is always there for me. I am my own person.*

Imagine your teenage daughter—or son—being able to think this way, rather than feeling the typical peer pressure where the untrained teen feels anxious, insecure, and is therefore easily influenced by a partner, other friends, or unscrupulous persons.

We also need to prepare children for exposure to sexual themes so common in the media and in the conversation of so many people. When children ask questions regarding sexual matters, wise parents will answer them, but only on their level of maturity. This should be done casually, being careful not to present the subject in a negative way. In fact, parents can speak of the appropriate setting for sex, in marriage, and convey to their children that it is something positive and wonderful when used as God intended. Please remember that no one else is likely to offer this kind of training to your children.

In addition, younger children need to be prepared for some of the language and attitudes they will encounter in school and at play. Then they will know that certain words are neither nice nor funny.

Violence in society and in the media presents a similar opportunity for parents. You want to protect your children from being exposed to it as much as possible. And yet, you know they are going to frequently encounter it, in adventure programs and certain fantasy cartoons on TV and also in the news. If they turn to such shows, you want them to have a rational and feeling response to them, rather than the desensitized reaction that many people have today. You want your children to be sensitive to the pain and plight of the victim, and to the needless recklessness and barbarianism of the perpetrator.

LOOK FOR TEACHABLE TIMES

Do you see the underlying theme of proactive parenting running through all of this? You don't wait until something terrible happens and then react. You anticipate. You prepare. You think ahead. You make sure your child is as ready as possible, and also as protected as necessary at each age level. The older your child is, the more that protection has to be within, since you cannot be present at all times. This is positive parenting.

This type of preparation and teaching cannot be structured like a business meeting. With children, you need to look for the teachable times. There are two general kinds of teachable moments. The first is when your child is inquisitive and asking about an issue. The advantage to this is that your child is already interested and is taking the initiative. This means she is motivated to learn and will almost always be responsive to what you are trying to teach. You need to watch for these times, for they are precious opportunities.

One of the most teachable times in a child's life is at the "why" stage, when you are bombarded with questions. You should be thankful when your child asks questions because this means she is open to your answers. However, this also means that you need to be available to your child enough of the time for such questions to arise naturally. We have heard so much about "quality time" in recent years. What some of these people forget is that a child's questions and needs may not arise in what the parent regards as "quality time." Adequate parenting means taking time when questions come.

The other highly teachable time is when your child feels close to you emotionally. One such favorite is bedtime, for you and your child can have a close and loving bond in this regular time of reading and talking and praying together. Bedtime is a great opportunity to meet emotional needs and also to offer training and guidance, in an atmosphere which a child will remember fondly.

As our children were growing up, Pat and I would often read to an individual child, sometimes a secular story or one from the Bible or a Christian book. I often made up stories which I could use to make a particular point I felt a child needed. We also read short devotional stories, to lead into conversation about spiritual values. As our children asked questions about the stories, we were delighted, for their questions were like royal invitations into their hearts. Many books have questions after each story, and these are helpful to parents, especially when a child doesn't comment on the story.

Bedtime was also a time we could nonchalantly mention something negative they might soon be encountering. Or a child could ask us about a difficulty they experienced. In this very relaxed setting, we could assure our children that they were free to come to us about any matter they wanted, that we were totally open to their needs.

RELEASING A CHILD

As our society becomes increasingly hazardous for our children, it is ever more important to know how and when to release them. I am not referring only to releasing them when they leave home as young adults. I mean all of the big and little times, as children proceed from one level of activity to another. We need to release them to greater levels of responsibility and independence. Some children will need to remain in a dependent situation for longer periods than others their own age. This can apply to the age for dating alone or for going to certain kinds of social occasions that the parent thinks the child is not yet ready for.

One way to deal with the continual process of releasing a child is to train him to understand the consequences of behavior. This is a gradual process that may accelerate when he enters the teen years. He must understand that privileges are dependent on responsible behavior. Be sure your teenager understands clearly that the more mature his behavior, the greater will be his privileges. You want to be able to say yes as much as possible but also to feel the freedom to say no when that is necessary. The more accustomed your teenager is to this equation of responsible behavior equaling privilege and the more he knows that you truly want him to have a happy life, the fewer problems you will have in deciding what is appropriate.

This behavior-privilege approach is not easy for parents. In fact, it takes courage, especially during adolescence. However, if you have trained your children in this way from their earliest years, it will be easier when they reach the teenage years. If your children are approaching adolescence, I hope you will read my book *How to Really Love Your Teenager*. The chapter "From Parent Control to Self-Control" discusses this issue in more depth.

Offering sufficient protection and granting appropriate release to a child is one of the most difficult challenges for parents today. On the one hand, we want to be sure our child can handle a situation before we allow her to be independent. However, we do not want her to harbor the notion that we are trying to hold her back or prevent her from becoming independent in a certain area. Wise parents assure a child that they want her to become independent as soon as possible. But a prudent parent also will tell her, "I always will be looking out for your safety and welfare. When you reach a maturity level that assures us you're able to look out just as well, then you're on your own there—though Dad [Mom] is always there to help."

Yes, protection and release go together. First, protection. Then release.

NOTE

1. Jennifer Braun, "Parents Make for Kids Who Read Better," *Chattanooga Times,* 18 June 1996, A–10.

Chapter Six

The Fourth Foundation Stone:
TRAINING IN ANGER MANAGEMENT

Everyone should be quick to listen, slow to speak and slow to become angry, for man's anger does not bring about the righteous life that God desires.

The young mother halted her shopping cart that had been turning down aisle after aisle and looked her son, about three, in the eye. Her voice was emphatic and deliberate: "Put . . . it . . . back!"

"But I *want* it!" her son whined. His grip tightened around the Ninja Turtles cereal box.

"Put it back!" Mom said louder. Her anger was rising. Author Daniel Goleman describes what happened next:

> At that moment the baby in her shopping cart seat dropped the jelly she had been mouthing. When it shattered on the floor the mother yelled, "That's it!" and, in a fury, slapped the baby, grabbed the three-year-old's box and slammed it onto the nearest shelf, scooped him up by the waist, and rushed down the aisle, the shopping cart careening perilously in front, the baby now crying, her son, his legs dangling, protesting, "Put me *down,* put me *down!*"[1]

Mishandled anger is at the root of most problems in our individual lives, in our homes, and in society. The reason for this is that appropriate ways of handling anger must be learned, since they do not come naturally. Mature management of anger needs to be taught at home, and yet this seldom happens today. Have you had any training in anger management? Probably not. And neither have most of the people you know.

Very few parents are aware that training a child to handle anger well is one of their most important responsibilities. Nor do parents seem to realize that training a child to manage anger maturely is the most difficult aspect of parenting.

Training our children in managing their anger is the fourth foundation stone in rearing children to maturity. Yet we seem confused as to how to do it. Perhaps that's because most of us misunderstand this emotion called *anger*—why we feel it, how we express it, and how we can change the way we deal with it. Unless parents know what anger is and how to handle it in appropriate ways, they will not be able to teach their children what to do when they feel angry. For, let's face it, we all feel more or less angry on a regular basis. But when children get angry, most parents respond to it in a wrong and destructive manner. The main reason for this is that the parents have never learned to manage their own anger. Their first challenge is to learn how to handle their own anger, to be able to "be . . . angry and sin not" (Ephesians 4:26 KJV), as the apostle Paul reminded us.

A LIFELONG THREAT

The primary lifelong threat to your child's well-being is anger. The extent to which your child learns to manage anger will determine some of the most important outcomes in his or her life. This includes respect for legitimate authority and the moral direction of life. Mismanaged anger can damage or destroy your child's life. It can cause or aggravate every present or potential problem your child may have, from poor grades to damaged relationships, depression, and possible suicide. It is imperative that you do all you can to safeguard your child now and in the future against an inappropriate handling of anger.

We can easily see evidences of poorly controlled anger in society. Violence erupts in every setting, including schools and churches and neighborhoods. However, training a child in anger management is not the responsibility of society. It is up to parents to carry out this long and difficult task. The tragedy is that this is not happening in most homes. In fact, most children are actually being taught to handle their anger in inappropriate and destructive ways—and they are learning these lessons at home from parents who don't realize what they are teaching. They are just behaving as they always have, in ways that they learned from their parents.

Uncontrolled anger exhibits itself in irrational behavior and violence. It usually takes away our ability to reason and has a destructive influence on a person's motivations. Anger directed at a young child is terrifying, especially when it comes from a parent. A child is defenseless against parental anger, and for this reason it is his greatest fear. If the parent does not learn to control his anger, as well as the child's, this fear will change to resentment and to anti-parent attitudes and behaviors.

Yes, it is true that anger has a positive side—when it is controlled and used to effect changes. There are situations in which we should feel a righteous anger, at behaviors and attitudes that are harming innocent people. But even in these, it has to be controlled and then channeled constructively.

To be able to employ anger positively is the goal, for parents and children alike. For this to happen, you first need to understand how the mind operates in its handling of anger.

THE WAYS WE RESPOND TO ANGER

We can respond to anger in only two ways—in actions and in words. Therefore, your children are quite limited in their expressions of anger. Both choices—behavioral and verbal—seem unpleasant to parents. If a young child expresses anger behaviorally, by banging his head, throwing toys, hitting or kicking, his behavior must be dealt with. If the child expresses anger verbally, it will almost certainly come across to the parent as disrespectful and inappropriate. Therefore, both means of expressing anger are usually unacceptable.

Only Two Choices

What a terrible dilemma for the child, who has only these two ways to vent his anger. He doesn't have the choice to hold it in forever. It has to come out in some form, sooner or later. No one knows how many people are depressed or sick or in prison because of suppressed childhood anger.

What a dilemma for parents! If we refuse to allow a child to express anger in any way at all, he must then push the anger deeper and deeper within, causing destructive problems later in life. If he expresses all his anger, either verbally or behaviorally, and it takes a destructive form, we punish him. As a result, he has no other choice but to suppress that anger in the future. Either way, he will never learn to handle anger maturely.

This is but another example of the punishment trap into which so many parents fall, thinking that punishment itself is the way to teach children how to handle anger. This is the very point at which parents need to be proactive rather than reactive. Instead of merely reacting to the anger and trying to make it go away, the wise parent will see the expression of anger as a teachable moment. Yes, the behavior may need to be controlled and changed, but this wise parent is more interested in the long-term lesson to be learned.

Another mistake many parents make, when a child is angry, is to explode and dump a load of their own anger on the child. But remember, a child is helpless in the face of parental anger. He has no defense against it.

Clearly, both child and parent face a dilemma. What is to be done? First, you want to keep in mind that a well-loved child is so much easier to discipline and train than one who does not feel loved. Therefore, *the first requirement in anger training is to keep your child's emotional tank full.*

Next, remember that training a child's anger responses is the most difficult part of parenting. One reason for this is that you probably find it difficult to keep yourself under emotional control while you are trying to train your child. It is a fact that children are immature and that they are going to handle their anger immaturely until they are trained otherwise. Until then, their natural and normal expressions of anger will tend to aggravate you.

Answers to a Dilemma

Since there are only two ways to express anger, you can control which of these two ways your child chooses. Which is better —verbal or behavioral expression? Verbal, of course.

Thus *the second requirement in anger training is to encourage your child to verbalize his anger.* In fact, the most mature way to handle anger is this:

- Verbally

- Pleasantly

- Resolving the anger with the person at whom you are angry, or . . .

- Finding ways to resolve it within yourself

When your child expresses his anger verbally, even though this may be unpleasant, he is well on his way to handling his anger in a mature way. Why? Because the requirement for the mature management of anger is to express it verbally. If you allow no expression of anger from your child, he will be forced to initially suppress the anger. But eventually, it will manifest itself subconsciously in passive-aggressive behavior (that is, indirect but negative behavior, a concept we will discuss shortly). *You cannot train your child in anger control until he first expresses the anger verbally.*

If your child comes at you with a great amount of anger and expresses it verbally, it will sound very unpleasant. Your typical response to this will be to become angry yourself—perhaps more angry than the child—and say something threatening like, "How dare you talk that way to me? I never, ever want to hear you talk like that again. Do you understand?"

If he is not going to express the anger verbally, this unfortunate child has two choices. He can obey you and "not talk that way again" and suppress the anger. In fact, he will suppress not only the anger he came to you with, but the anger you have provoked in him with your own unpleasantness. This is a sure way to make your child passive aggressive. The other choice your child has is to disobey you and to let the anger out behaviorally. Then you really have a problem!

You cannot train your child to manage his anger unless you teach him to express it verbally.[2] If you refuse to do this, your child will never learn to control anger in a mature way. This is the punishment trap in full display, as it produces anti-parent and antiauthority attitudes and feelings in children. Unfortunately, this is the scene in most homes today.

ANGER AND PASSIVE-AGGRESSIVE BEHAVIOR

Janet's Story

John and Pam had been having severe marital problems and thought that perhaps a child would bring them closer together. Janet was the result of this hope. She was calm, easy to manage, and did well in school and with friends. She was a sweet child who delighted in making others happy.

Although they could not have asked for a lovelier daughter, John and Pam did not resolve their own troubled relationship. They tried counseling for a short while, but that ended when Pam began working outside the home when Janet went to school. Within the year, the marital difficulties became so severe that John and Pam separated. Janet stayed with her mother and appeared to be unaffected by the change. She told people that her parents were living apart for a short time and would be together again soon.

Six months later, John and Pam decided to divorce. At this point Janet showed visible reaction, with her concentration and school work being affected. She became withdrawn from her peers and important adults in her life. At home she would cry and beg her mother not to let the divorce happen. At first Pam was sympathetic but later responded with impatience and eventually a good deal of anger. "The divorce is going to happen," she told Janet, "and you will just have to get used to it."

Janet never again talked about the divorce, and began again doing well in school and other activities. However, her anger continued to seethe and smolder, and by adolescence it was emerging as classical passive-aggressive behavior. Her grades fell dramatically and she behaved in a hostile way toward her parents and other adults. Then she was caught shoplifting. Soon after, she became pregnant and had an abortion.

At this point, Pam placed Janet in counseling, though she expected Janet to be uncooperative. To Pam's surprise, Janet appreciated the genuine concern she felt in the counseling sessions. Since by nature she was a sweet and cooperative child, this part of her personality soon reappeared and she made excellent progress. She suspected that her parents' divorce had much to do with her bad behavior, but she was surprised at the rage she had held within for so many years.

Janet did well in counseling and eventually learned to relate in a loving way to her parents and also to regain her poise with other people. She is one of the fortunate ones who received help in time to enable her to have a happy adult life. Her story underscores the far-reaching effects divorce can have on children. The most overlooked of these is their anger, which so often is not attended to by parents who are dealing with their own agendas of sadness and anger and adjustment to a new way of life. Because their children *appear* to be doing well, they ignore what is probably happening just beneath the surface.

What Is Passive Aggression?

Passive-aggressive behavior is the subconscious determination to do exactly the opposite of what is expected. Put in another way, it is the subconscious motivation to do the opposite of what the authority figure (parent, teacher, employer, spouse) wants one to do. It is a subtle kind of aggression, an underhanded way of moving against another person. It involves manipulation of others to get one's own selfish way.

Janet demonstrated classic passive-aggressive behavior in an effort to express her anger. Not able to talk about her hurt and anger, she found passive ways to express it, often subconsciously.

The purpose of passive-aggressive behavior is to upset and anger the parent or authority figure. You need to remember that this is a subconscious process; the child does not know, or is not fully aware of, why he is doing it. He may seem as baffled as the

parents. This happens in all homes. And, this misunderstood behavior is one reason why children with all types of problems
come from every kind of home, even the fine ones. Most parents
do not recognize or understand passive-aggressive behavior.

While verbal and controlled (pleasant) expressions form
the most mature way to handle anger—they usually lead to resolving the anger—passive aggression is the worst way to manage
anger. Passive-aggressive behavior is vicious, subtle, and everywhere. It has harmed and destroyed more lives than almost any
other means. It is the product of poor parenting and is avoidable if
parents provide good training in the mature management of anger.

We see a typical case of adolescent passive aggression in
sixteen-year-old Jerry, who is quite intelligent and has no learning
problems. He wants to make good grades and works hard to do
just that. But he confuses everyone by bringing home poor
grades, leaving both him and his parents at a loss. How could this
intelligent child who studies hard make such low grades? Jerry is
angry with his parents and needs to express his anger. So he does
the opposite of what his parents want. Jerry is not aware that he is
doing this to spite his parents, but he acts this way nonetheless.
Until his parents understand the reasons for this baffling but common problem, whatever they try will make the situation worse.

RECOGNIZING PASSIVE-AGGRESSIVE BEHAVIOR

Signs of Passive-Aggressive Behavior

There are three ways that parents can know if they are
dealing with passive aggression.

- The behavior seems to make no sense. His parents knew
  Jerry wanted to earn good grades, so they could not
  understand why he would choose to act this way.

- Nothing parents do will correct the behavior. Since the
  purpose of the behavior is to upset authority figures,
  nothing will work. Jerry's parents tried rewarding him
  for good grades. They tried punishing him when the
  grades were poor. Subconsciously, Jerry made sure

nothing would work, because his underlying purpose was to upset his parents.

• The child is the one who is hurt the most. It was Jerry who suffered from the poor grades. And yet the behavior went on.

Recognizing Normal and Abnormal Passive-Aggressive Behavior

Passive-aggressive behavior is normal in only one stage of a child's life—early adolescence, between ages thirteen and fifteen. Even then, it is normal only if it does not cause harm to anyone. Most young teens go through this stage of confusion and rebellion in order to reach adult maturity. During this stage, they must learn how to handle anger in a mature fashion, or they will become permanently passive-aggressive adults who have destructive relationships in every sphere of life.

Decades ago, when young people acted out during the normally rebellious stage, their choices were limited to activities that were aggravating but relatively harmless. They may have rolled trees with toilet paper or upset outhouses. But those exploits are a far cry from the present dangers of drugs, violence, crime, sexual activity, or suicide. Today we see unscrupulous and evil persons taking advantage of these normal drives in our youth, and reaping huge profits by making available catastrophic temptations for children in the form of guns, alcohol, drugs, pornography, and illicit sex.

Parents need to learn to distinguish between harmless passive-aggressive behavior and abnormal behavior. A fourteen-year-old's messy room is harmless and can be tolerated. Smoking pot is potentially life-threatening and cannot be tolerated. Finding ways to direct this normal passive-aggressive stage is a real challenge for parents, but doable, since there are many positive ways to satisfy a young teen's desire for excitement and danger. Strenuous physical activities, such as rope courses, mountain climbing, and biking, as well as team and individual sports, are great ways to direct the adolescent energy. This stage of life should be both healthy and exciting as the young person begins to learn to be self-confident and self-sufficient in the adult world.

MOVING TOWARD MATURITY

Anger Management by Age Seventeen

Your goal is to train your child to manage her anger by the time she is seventeen years old. Only by learning mature and acceptable ways to handle anger can she leave the early-teen passive-aggressive stage. The sad truth is that many adults have never left that stage, because they were never taught to understand or manage their anger.

The majority of parents make the mistake of thinking that all expressions of anger are wrong and must be disciplined out of a child. But this will not train a child to handle anger in constructive ways. Therefore, the child carries into adulthood inappropriate ways of handling anger, setting the stage for many of life's problems, such as college failure, employment difficulties, and marital stresses. Parents who do not want their child to become the victim of his own anger need to train the child to manage that anger well.

Although you begin anger management training when your child is very young, you shouldn't expect to see evidence of maturity in this area until she is six or seven years old. Remember, your child has only two options for expressing anger—her words and actions. When she vents anger in words, you can train her toward managing that anger well. Before age six or seven, your most important task is to keep passive-aggressive anger from becoming the controlling factor in her expression of anger. An empty emotional tank is fertile ground for passive-aggressive anger. By keeping your child's emotional tank filled with unconditional love, you can prepare her to progress in managing anger verbally. She will not need to express her anger behaviorally, in effect asking, "Do you love me?"

The Anger Ladder

The concept of an anger ladder can help you see the goal in teaching our children to manage their anger. The anger ladder begins on the lower rungs with the least effective forms of anger management and moves to increasingly effective forms of dealing

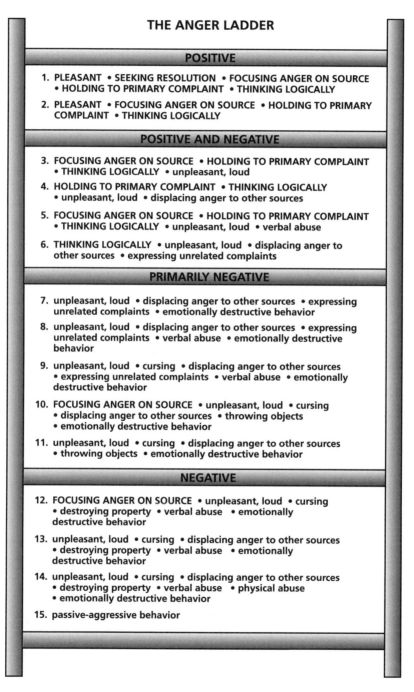

THE ANGER LADDER

POSITIVE

1. PLEASANT • SEEKING RESOLUTION • FOCUSING ANGER ON SOURCE • HOLDING TO PRIMARY COMPLAINT • THINKING LOGICALLY

2. PLEASANT • FOCUSING ANGER ON SOURCE • HOLDING TO PRIMARY COMPLAINT • THINKING LOGICALLY

POSITIVE AND NEGATIVE

3. FOCUSING ANGER ON SOURCE • HOLDING TO PRIMARY COMPLAINT • THINKING LOGICALLY • unpleasant, loud

4. HOLDING TO PRIMARY COMPLAINT • THINKING LOGICALLY • unpleasant, loud • displacing anger to other sources

5. FOCUSING ANGER ON SOURCE • HOLDING TO PRIMARY COMPLAINT • THINKING LOGICALLY • unpleasant, loud • verbal abuse

6. THINKING LOGICALLY • unpleasant, loud • displacing anger to other sources • expressing unrelated complaints

PRIMARILY NEGATIVE

7. unpleasant, loud • displacing anger to other sources • expressing unrelated complaints • emotionally destructive behavior

8. unpleasant, loud • displacing anger to other sources • expressing unrelated complaints • verbal abuse • emotionally destructive behavior

9. unpleasant, loud • cursing • displacing anger to other sources • expressing unrelated complaints • verbal abuse • emotionally destructive behavior

10. FOCUSING ANGER ON SOURCE • unpleasant, loud • cursing • displacing anger to other sources • throwing objects • emotionally destructive behavior

11. unpleasant, loud • cursing • displacing anger to other sources • throwing objects • emotionally destructive behavior

NEGATIVE

12. FOCUSING ANGER ON SOURCE • unpleasant, loud • cursing • destroying property • verbal abuse • emotionally destructive behavior

13. unpleasant, loud • cursing • displacing anger to other sources • destroying property • verbal abuse • emotionally destructive behavior

14. unpleasant, loud • cursing • displacing anger to other sources • destroying property • verbal abuse • physical abuse • emotionally destructive behavior

15. passive-aggressive behavior

Note: Phrases in capital letters indicate positive ways to express anger feelings.
SOURCE: Ross Campbell, *Kids in Danger* (Colorado Springs: Chariot Victor, 1999), 69.

with one's anger. Young children will likely be at the very bottom of that ladder. Your goal is to work with them, helping them to climb from one rung to the next as they move from passive-aggressive behavior and verbal abuse to more positive ways of handling anger. This will take years of training and much patience, since progress is usually in small increments.

Study the anger ladder, shown on page 101. Notice that passive-aggressive behavior is at the very bottom of the ladder. This represents unmanageable behavior. Remember, this is normal only in the early teen years, and then in expressions that do not hurt other people. You need to work with a child of any age to see that there is progress but without expecting immediate or rapid results. Your child can climb only one rung at a time, and may wait a while before progressing to the next rung.

Your goal is for your child to move toward the best forms of verbal expression of anger. However, to do this means that you will have to put up with some unacceptable and disrespectful forms of expression, or you run the risk of making your child suppress all anger which will come out later in behaviors that are unacceptable.

Some "Self-Talk"

I have often had to resort to self-talk when confronted with verbal anger from one of my children. I would remind myself of the positives in the way he was verbalizing his anger, and that he was at a higher level than he was a year ago. Also, I would remind myself that by verbalizing, he was not running the risk of internalizing and becoming passive aggressive. Such a parental attitude may seem permissive. However, we need to remember that immature children of any age will express anger in immature ways. If we as parents get upset and force them to stop venting their anger verbally, we cannot expect to train them in more mature forms of expression.

When your child gets angry, it is good to ask yourself, "Is she usually respectful? Usually cooperative?" If your child has been given the proper emotional nurture, your answer will be yes. If this is the case, and your child brings her verbal anger to you, she is providing you a golden opportunity to train her and help her move up the ladder to more mature anger expressions.

Is this asking too much—to feel grateful when your child expresses anger? And also to control your own anger? Of course this is not easy, but it is an exercise that will force you to mature as well. You need to always keep in mind your goal of saving untold heartaches and problems in the future for your child, your family, and yourself.

This may seem confusing to you. However, allowing your child to bring his anger to you verbally when he is upset about a particular problem will provide you an opportunity to train him. But be sure to control yourself as your child expresses his anger verbally.

There are children who verbalize anger most of the time and for trivial reasons. They may be doing this to manipulate their parents and get their own way. Angry verbal expressions motivated by a desire to upset and hurt others are inappropriate and must be corrected. Parents need to deal with those words as they do with any misbehavior, as we discussed in chapter 4. But in the correction, they should practice the basic parental parameters: Be patient but firm.

If your child is ventilating his anger for no discernible reason, or simply to manipulate you, handle his response like any other misbehavior. However, even with unacceptable ventilation, you need to use appropriate discipline, being careful not to dump your anger on your child. Always remain pleasant but firm.

Effective Anger Training

When your child brings normal and occasional anger to you, he is also bringing himself to be trained. However, this training cannot take place until you have both calmed down and reestablished good feelings. In order to be effective, the training should be done as soon after the incident as possible. You need to do the following three things to help him deal with his anger in a positive way:

- Let him know that you are not going to condemn him. He may already feel very guilty, especially if he is a child who wants to please. If you condemn him, he might never again express his anger, and you would not be able to help him climb the anger ladder to more positive ways of handling disagreements. He needs to know that you accept him as a person who has feelings, and that you want to know those feelings. When he is happy you want to know it, and when he is sad or angry, you also want to know.

• Focus on the things he did right. By bringing verbal anger to you, he has done some right things and avoided some harmful ones. He didn't hit his little brother or kick the dog. He told you he was angry and this is what you want.

• Help him understand how he can express his anger more positively the next time. By using requests rather than commands, you let him know that the responsibility is his and that you expect him to handle it. This won't happen overnight, but you will begin to see a gradual maturing toward your goal, as he moves up the ladder to maturity.

RESOLVING ANGER THROUGH FORGIVENESS

Modeling Forgiveness

In the course of family life, offenses do happen and every person at times should say those difficult words, "I am sorry. Will you forgive me?" Because we parents are not paragons of perfection, on occasion we too need to ask for forgiveness—from each other, from friends and business associates, and also from our children.

Our children may be angry because they believe we have acted unfairly toward them. Yes, there are times when we wrong our children and anger them. There are times when we feel that we are in the right, on an adult level, when they think we are very much in the wrong, from a child's perspective. For after all, that is what they are dealing with—the way a child looks at life. If we want a growing, love relationship with our children, whether they are age two or twenty, we need to consider the way they look at life and at themselves. And if we have offended them, even if our offense was not intentional, we will need to apologize and ask forgiveness.

One mother I know has found it appropriate to tell her children every so often, "If I do or say things that really upset you, I wish you would tell me. Not next year, but that day or the next."

She used to say this when they were at home growing up, and now has said it to her adult children, since the opportunity for misunderstanding still presents itself once in a while. As adults, we are dealing with life on more levels than growing children are. As we try to take care of so many details every day, we can easily say or do something that is translated as less than respectful or loving toward their feelings.

If a child takes advantage of the invitation to vent to the parent on a very regular basis, there is probably something wrong with the personal dynamics in the family. But, if it happens two or three times a year, a parent should take it as a vote of confidence that the child feels free to air a grievance as part of the ongoing love shared in the family.

Because we are dealing every day with a child's perceptions of life, we may need to ask for forgiveness—not always for the act itself but for our insensitivity to our child's feelings. Or, we may take the occasion to explain some facts about life or about our own motivations that we have never before discussed with this child. Either way, it is time for coming closer together.

Teaching Forgiveness

Forgiveness is closely aligned with expressions of anger. We teach forgiveness to our children not only by modeling it in the family, but also by how we respond to offenses that come from outside the household, and by how we talk with them about Christian forgiveness.

Forgiveness has many definitions, but one that I like is this: Forgiveness is giving up the right to get even. It is a determination to let go of the pain and grief and hurt. Some people say that we should not forgive unless the other person is repentant, but Scripture does not bear this out. We are instructed to forgive others as we are forgiven—seventy times seven (Matthew 18:22 KJV). We are also told to forgive as Christ has forgiven us (Ephesians 4:32).

However, we must be prepared to forgive before we can genuinely do so. If we are still in a state of anger and fury, we are not ready to forgive, and our attempt to do so will be fruitless. We will remain in the same state of agitation.

An offense and a need for forgiveness is not always a personal matter between two people. There are times when life just cannot get back to any semblance of normality until some resolution has been reached. To do this may require the involvement of one or more outside persons. Jesus spoke to this matter during His ministry, and in Matthew 18:15–20 we read the progression of steps to take in order to come to a resolution when there has been a serious offense.

Forgiveness is a spiritual matter and must be handled as any other spiritual experience—with the help of the Lord. As we pray about our need to forgive, God will ease our pain and discomfort, but usually slowly and gradually. In fact, when people are severely wronged, it often takes up to three years before they are ready to forgive fully. We know we have reached this point when the thought of the offending person does not bring feelings of vengeance. Then we are ready to forgive and free ourselves of the negative thoughts and feelings surrounding that person.

Such total forgiveness is a wonderfully freeing experience, and it is critical for healing and for maintaining a healthy spiritual life.

DO NOT DUMP YOUR ANGER ON YOUR CHILD

The more effectively you deal with anger at home—your own and your child's—the less it will extend outside the home. If you fail to train your child at home, her passive-aggressive behavior will generalize outside the home and cause embarrassing and potentially dangerous problems. You certainly want to keep the annoyances of normal passive-aggressive behavior inside the home.

One important trick of the trade is to refuse to dump your anger on your child. One method to help you prevent this disastrous habit is to make a pledge to yourself as you go to bed at night. Write in a notebook, "I will not dump my anger on my child for the next twenty-four hours." Then the next night, write the same thing in your notebook and date it. You will also want to record how you did in managing your own anger. If you lost it and dumped your anger on your child, write it down. Also, note the circumstances under which this happened. Then, make a simple plan to help you do better the next day. Finally, make a renewed promise to try to handle your anger well for the next day.

We all need the help of our heavenly Father in this difficult area. Prayer is a crucial part of managing our anger well. You may find it helpful to write your prayers so that you can refer to them when you are in a nonspiritual mood and find that prayer is difficult. You may also want to write down some verses from the Bible to give you help in hard times. Our heavenly Father cares, and He will help when we rely fully on Him.

If you are trying to become a more pleasant and less angry parent, your child will know it and will deeply appreciate your effort. And you will know that you are contributing to your child's happiness and productivity for the rest of his life.

Always keep in mind that the most important part of training children to manage anger is your unconditional love for them. When they feel confident in your love, they will be responsive to your training and far more likely to reach your goal of helping them to be emotionally mature by the time they are in their late teens.

NOTES

1. Daniel Goleman, *Emotional Intelligence* (New York: Bantam, 1995), 61.
2. For more tips on letting a child express anger verbally, see Gary Chapman and Ross Campbell, *The Five Love Languages of Children* (Chicago: Northfield, 1997), 156-57. Also see Ross Campbell, *Kids in Danger: Disarming the Destructive Power in Your Child* (Colorado Springs: Chariot Victor, 1999).

Chapter Seven

The Media Versus Parents

Love the Lord your God with all your heart and with all your soul and with all your mind and with all your strength.
MARK 12:30

We have four national television networks broadcasting in our area: ABC, NBC, CBS, and Fox. On a day when I wanted to watch the final game of the World Series, I didn't know which channel was carrying it, so I flipped through the four to find it.

On the first channel, I watched as one couple was seducing another couple into wife-swapping. Repulsed, I went to the next, where two homosexuals were having an in-your-face "love" affair. Repulsed again, I switched to the third channel where I had the opportunity to see a woman be terrorized with unspeakably sadistic violence. On the fourth try, I found the game. However, several times during the game, beer commercials with provocative sexual messages were shown. All of this happened in a time frame when children were watching television.

I begin with television, but we all know that the media we are up against as parents include movies, video games, computers with Internet access to adult web sites, and print. All parents are aware of the potential dangers and many are troubled by them. And yet, in most homes the television is on several hours a day, and children ages two through five watch TV an average of thirteen hours Monday through Friday.[1]

The powers that be, especially political leaders, make promises to help control the media, and yet change is slow and resisted by Hollywood studios and many at the networks. The so-called "V-chip," the new computer chip in television sets that can block out programs that feature violence or sex, will be of some help. Yet the fact that parents need such a filter reveals how much television has become a wilderness when it comes to regular TV viewing. (Cable TV is much less regulated.) Critics believe the V-chip will be an excuse for producers to create more violent or adult-theme programs because children supposedly will never see those shows. As a result, we can expect more violence and sexual scenes on television. Of course, these chips are available only when you buy a new TV set; millions of existing TVs provide no such protection for our children.

The result is that the best of parents are losing the battle and many don't know why. The forms of entertainment available today are rendering parenting methods of the past ineffective and even a problem in themselves. As children are desensitized to the unhealthy messages of the media and then enter the ages of normal passive aggressive behavior, they have many more destructive outlets available.

Peter Gibbon, a research associate at Harvard University's Graduate School of Education, lamented that television offers young people so little to admire. Also, it offers our children too many choices on a daily basis.

> As parents, we need to realize that there are dangers that come with too many choices and too few guides. We need to remind ourselves that their well-being depends not only on nutrition, sunlight, and exercise; on friendship, work, and love, but also on *how they see the world*. Subtly and powerfully, the media helps shape their world view.
>
> The media has a liberal bias, but its central bias is toward bad news. Accidents, crimes, conflict, and scandal are interest-

ing. Normality is boring. The prevalence of bad news and the power of the image encourage children—and us—to overestimate the chance of an accident, the risk of disease, the rate of violence, the frequency of marital infidelity . . .

In a wired world with no restraint, the media can misinform us. It can also make us suspicious, fearful, and cynical. It can lead us to lose faith in our nation, repudiate our past, question our leaders, and cease to believe in progress. . . .

Hovering in the background are secularism—which suggests that human beings are self-sufficient and do not need God—and modernism, a complex artistic and literary movement that repudiates structure, form and conventional values.

Finally, in an age of instant communication, in which there is little time for reflection, accuracy, balance or integrity, the media creates the impression that sleaze is everywhere, that nothing is sacred, that no one is noble, and that there are no heroes.[2]

Television is only one medium but a pervasive one, with 99 percent of American households having at least one TV set and 36 percent having three sets.[3] Television and its media brothers are influencing a changing culture. We must train our precious ones to cope with these harmful messages. Clearly, we need a new approach to parenting. There is too much at stake—not only our children's ability to be decent, mentally healthy people but also, as they grow into adults, the future of our society.

CORRUPTING MESSAGES ACROSS THE MEDIA

The Internet

With all its exciting possibilities that open a wider world to us, the Internet can pose a great danger to children and teens. Parents who care about their children cannot take anything for granted about how and when their children are utilizing the Internet. This matter is serious enough that some parents need to think about the location of their home computers. Most children will not access lewd and violent material when they are in the same room with older family members. Also, to offer children private access to the Internet, even when they are using it in positive ways, can draw them away from time they should be spending with the family.

Unfortunately, too many parents are not paying attention, and their children are seeing depraved sexual material, outrageous violence, and information about guns and bombs. We need appropriate safeguards to protect and guide our children during their growing years. All parents who have computers need to learn how to use them as well as their children do, so that they can monitor what is going on in their homes.

One potentially dangerous area of the Internet is the chat room. Some of these are supervised and others are not. In a letter to *Good Housekeeping* magazine, Sarah from Pennsylvania wrote, "I am sixteen years old, but I have never ventured into one of those [unsupervised] teen chat rooms. I cannot tolerate the rude comments and atrocious grammar. But not all chat rooms are bad. I belong to one that tolerates no profanity. There is always an operator there to supervise, and it's safe for kids of all ages."[4]

Sarah has the right idea, a supervised chat room with reasonable rules. Yet even that will not assure your child's protection from a slew of conflicting and sometimes immoral messages. And some unsupervised chat rooms have a following among teens who feel "anything goes" is part of growing up. For instance, Katherine of Michigan wrote *Good Housekeeping,* "I'm seventeen years old and have been online since I was eleven. I have run into just about as many fifteen-year-old boys online who like to talk dirty as I have in school and elsewhere. But more often, I have had mind-opening discussions with people who have similar interests. No doubt teenagers speak in graphic detail about sex in some chat rooms—but they also do this on playgrounds."[5]

The most frightening aspect of teens being online is that some become engrossed with adults who are out to take advantage of them. Patricia, a mother on the West Coast, wrote, "When we had online services, our then thirteen-year-old daughter would be glued to the computer for hours. At first we thought perhaps she might be gaining some valuable experience. Then the trouble began. She would only 'chat' with the door shut, and she'd talk about chat room friends with names like Pimp Dog. Male callers would refuse to identify themselves. Others would hang up when an adult answered. What frightened us most was that our daughter arranged for a date she'd got through a chat room to come to our home while we weren't there."[6]

The number of teenagers entering chat rooms and being solicited to meet adults has increased, as have reports of juveniles being coaxed into rendezvous with adult strangers with selfish, sometimes evil intentions. Recently a fourteen-year-old girl from Tennessee corresponded with a thirty-six-year-old man from Nebraska in a chat room. He presented himself as being nineteen and arranged to meet her secretly. When they met, he kidnapped and raped her.[7]

Television and Video Violence

We have noted how the increasing level of violent content has brought about the V-chip in an effort to lock out offensive programs. Television content has become so adult in nature that the industry adopted a rating system in 1997; now programs range from TV-G to TV-MA (mature audiences only) and include the added designations of V, S, L and D for violence, sex, crude language, and dialogue containing sexual themes, respectively.

Television programs do influence our children's behavior. I once heard a presentation by Dr. David Walsh, executive director of the National Institute on Media and the Family. He had with him a study, caught on videotape, of children watching and responding to TV shows. During his presentation, he showed a video clip from the study. A group of four- and five-year-olds were seated before a television set, their parents observing them behind one-way mirrors. First the children saw a cartoon of Barney, who was dancing. After a few minutes, the children were also dancing, imitating Barney. The parents smiled in amusement.

Then the video changed to the Power Rangers, who were using karate chops, leg kicks, and delivering damaging blows to their foes. Within a short time, all but one or two children were likewise delivering hurtful blows to each other. One girl who at first withdrew soon was engaged in attempting to harm her classmates. This time, the parents were in shock, not only at the behavior of their children, but also at the clear demonstration of the effects of watching violence.

This demonstration took just a few minutes. Imagine the influence on children who watch violent programs and videos on a regular basis.

Clearly the degree and grossness of violence on TV and in videos is increasing. The TV programmers, wishing to hold children's attention, must overcome sensitization to violence. As the children are desensitized to the degree of violence, scenes have to be made more and more shocking and destructive. I spent eight years in the U.S. Navy, have practiced medicine in the most primitive areas of the world, and I used to think that I had seen it all. Was I wrong! However, people who become desensitized are unaware of the depth of depravity that has crept into our everyday life.

Many types of violence displayed on TV are acts that few would think of committing. Yet the copycat phenomenon proves that these unthinkable acts of barbarism are influencing the behavior in our society to a devastating degree. After highly publicized shootings at schools, for instance, look at the acts of shooting classmates at school and copycat plans for similar acts appearing online.

Only previously viewed acts of this kind could have influenced a child to commit such atrocities. This was amply shown in a 1993 study at the Penn State University Medical School, which demonstrated the relationship between aggressive and disobedient behavior of children and the number of hours they spent watching television. The more hours that the children watched television, the more aggressive and impulsive their behavior became. The American Academy of Pediatricians, in a 1990 study, established the fact that watching television twenty-five hours a week produced or increased aggressive behavior, obesity in children, and disturbances in sleep.[8] How ironic that most civilized countries protect their people from being exposed to the destructive and corrupting influences of violence in the media. We do not.

Video Games

Violence-oriented video games not only teach children the skills to kill like soldiers do, but they also teach them to enjoy it. Before a Senate panel, this issue was spoken to by Lt. Colonel David Grossman, a psychologist who taught military psychology at the U.S. Military Academy at West Point. He said that the video games go far beyond movies in influencing youngsters, because they actually train people to shoot. "These are true simulators that are also used by the armed forces to train soldiers. The military doesn't spend millions on these video games just for the heck of it. They do it because it works. For example, the game Doom is considered an excellent tactical training device for the Marine Corps."[9]

Like television, video games have had to adopt a rating system. Those with graphic and ongoing violence contain warning labels ranging from "teen" to "adults only." The teen category (suggested for children thirteen and older) includes games that "may contain violent content, mild or strong language, and/or suggestive themes" and includes such titles as "Body Harvest" and "Deadly Arts." The "mature" category is products that "may include more intense violence or language than products in the teen category. In addition, these titles may include mature sexual themes."[10] Such popular games as "Duke Nukem" and "Doom" carry the "mature" label.

While most video stores do not rent "adult only" games, many carry the other two labels and do not always check children's ages. Parents need to be alert to the labels and specific descriptions on the back of the game packages their children are thinking of renting or buying.

Movies, Magazines, and Sexual Messages

The overemphasis on sex, actually an obsession with sex, becomes a major negative influence on children. The sexual images and messages usually are corrupting, as sex is depicted as superficial, humorous, or violent, with little or no concern for or commitment to the sexual partner. Sexual relations in the media usually occur between unmarried people, and in a promiscuous, immature, and irresponsible manner.

Although children under seventeen supposedly are not allowed without their parents in theaters showing R-rated movies, surveys by local newspapers as well as national publications like *USA Today* have shown it is easy for children to enter multiscreen theaters, where cashiers don't check age—or where curious teens buying a PG ticket can slip into a theater showing an R-rated movie. Meanwhile, both cable TV and video tapes allow children to watch all sorts of sexual exploits.

In addition, in-your-face homosexual encounters are depicted increasingly in movies, as well as on television. Although homosexual lifestyles are certainly anti-family and anti-Christian, the shows presenting them show them as light and meaningless and normal. We need to ask what this is doing to the attitudes of children about commitment, dedication, and sacrifice for family.

Furthermore, the so-called "soft-porn" of *Playboy* and *Penthouse* now finds legitimacy, even being offered by subscription houses during their annual publishing sweepstakes drives. These magazines and harder pornographic fare can be found in convenience stores, and copies often find their way into children's hands.

Not long ago, I counseled Frank, a thirty-five-year-old with a deep sense of values. Yet this serious and tenderhearted adult was having problems with anxiety, depression, and relationships with the opposite sex. I discovered that another major problem for Frank was guilt, which came from exposure to sexually explicit material as a young teen. This occurred at the home of his friend Jack, whose mother would give the boys pornographic materials and also watch pay-per-view programs with them. Frank's parents were unaware of what was happening and would have take action had Frank told them.

His story is not unusual. Helping Frank took considerable time, but he was eventually healed from this devastating affliction. He came to understand the false guilt that was plaguing his ability to relate normally to women. He began dating and eventually married. Now Frank and his wife, Alice, have a wonderful family and some good friendships with other couples.

Exposure to sexually depraved scenes produces a feeling of unworthiness. Sexual purity is a precious possession which we want to safeguard, for our children and ourselves. Yes, forgiveness by our heavenly Father will "cleanse us from all unrighteousness" (1 John 1:9 NASB), but how much better to have protected a child in the first place.

CORRUPTING MESSAGES ABOUT INTEGRITY

As you watch television with your child, consider what the programs are teaching about integrity. You will remember that the three elements of integrity are telling the truth, keeping one's promises, and taking responsibility for one's own behavior. A majority of situation comedies on television ridicule integrity, display a disrespect for the truth, and often honor the person who lies. You will hear the words "I promise" spoken often in sitcoms, as characters promise things they either can't or don't intend to fulfill.

The most glaring example of broken promises on TV is toward marriage vows. Marriage is often depicted as a negative, as something that restrains us and prevents our happiness. As a consequence, many children come to believe that marriage is a bygone institution, except when they decide to have children. Of course, this attitude encourages premarital and extramarital sex, both of which are regularly portrayed on screen. How many scenes of writhing and panting does a child need to see before he believes that casual sex is the norm?

Among the most popular programs with children have been *The Simpsons* and cable TV's *Beavis and Butthead.* Both of them show total disrespect for authority, depicting parents and other authority figures as stupid, incompetent, and worthy of ridicule and aggression. Other programs offer these themes in a more moderate fashion, but a similar message comes across. Through what they experience from the media, children are being radically influenced in their attitudes toward basic right and wrong, and values about family and spiritual matters. How can our society survive when our children are being trained to be exactly opposite of what we want them to be? And, I might add, trained that way because their parents are passively allowing it.

We are seeing a few exceptions today, programs such as *Touched by an Angel* and *Promised Land,* both of which include prayer, the belief in a loving and just God, and people who eventually seek after Him. But we have to turn off so many other programs to get to the good ones.

THE PROPAGANDA OF MOVIES

Screenwriter Coleman Luck says that evangelical Christians and Hollywood do not understand each other. He claims that most evangelical Christians believe that Hollywood is motivated completely by money. While that is important, many producers and actors participate because of their convictions and desire to convey key messages. They believe passionately in their films, and they misunderstand and misrepresent Christianity.

> The only forms of Christianity Hollywood understands are Catholicism and right-wing conservative politics dressed in religious terminology. . . . Hollywood is guilty of ugly and cheap stereotypes of people of faith. If they tried those stereotypes with sexual orientation or gender or race they would be justifiably castigated.[11]

Movies convey clear messages, some of which are important, dealing with such themes as racism *(In the Heat of the Night, Schindler's List)*, the futility of war *(Saving Private Ryan)* and, on rare occasions, faith *(Chariots of Fire)*. But more often they include anti-Christian or anti-family propaganda. Box office receipts indicate that wholesome films make much more money than those pandering to sexual interests and violence. Luck is right to some degree about the convictions and stereotypes pedaled by filmmakers. If money were the only motivator, would not filmmakers produce what would earn the most? We can have little doubt that many of these talented people are doing their part in social engineering, trying to bring about a society that Christians find dangerous, especially for children.

PARENTS IN A QUANDARY

In many homes, the television set is given a prominent place and when no one is watching, the set provides background noise. In two-thirds of homes, the television is on during at least one meal. Children brought up in this kind of environment can become addicted to the sound itself, so that they feel uncomfortable when they are in a quiet surrounding. This impacts not only their inner development but also their behavior in places where they should be quiet, such as school and church.

Compared with the hours they spend watching television, children spend little time on the genuinely important areas of their lives. The average school age child, for example, spends half an hour each week with her father, two and one-half hours with her mother, five hours per week doing homework, and nearly half an hour reading outside of school assignments.[12] Compare this with thirteen hours each week watching television.

We parents allow this extensive viewing for many reasons, rarely thinking about the power of television. Yet TV can consume our children's thoughts and actions as much as it consumes their time. While most children have a difficult time concentrating on important tasks such as studying, reading, or learning through listening to a teacher, parent, or minister, these same children become totally absorbed with a TV program. Can we call this addiction? I think so. When children who watch TV regularly are kept from the TV set, they often go through the symptoms of withdrawal. They become anxious, nervous, angry, easily frustrated, and difficult to relate to. After a time of being away from the television set, they gradually regain their stability and ability to react normally to stress.

Many parents are not paying enough attention to the technology or content of the media today, but their children are very savvy about both. It is time for these parents to make the effort to catch up with their kids and find out what is going on. Our society is no place for complacency about what is going into the minds and hearts and nervous systems of children.

Also, many parents are failing to make connections between what goes into the consciousness of our children and what comes out in behavior and attitudes. Parents don't pay sufficient attention to what their children are involved in, letting their children decide what to do. Later, if trouble results, some parents wonder what went wrong. If these parents would stop to compare the amount of time they spend with their children with the amount of time the children are influenced by media and culture, many parents would find out that they are coming in last.

WHAT CAN WE AS PARENTS DO?

With this pervasive influence of the media and a changing culture, we need a strong, active approach to parenting. That means a proactive approach, not a reactive one. We can train our precious ones to cope with the harmful and corrupting messages that are all around them. There is too much at stake for us not to do so.

Our overall goal as parents is to nurture, to train, and to protect. Let me remind you that no effort to train and protect against unwanted entertainment forms will succeed if we do not first nurture our children. We must keep our children's emotional tanks full of unconditional love if the rest of our efforts are to succeed. And then we must be in control of our child's access to outside influences in order to train him. Finally, we must protect him from the unwholesome messages of this anti-parent and anti-child society.

Using the Media for Good

We need not abandon all modern media. Instead, we can use them to help us convey important messages to our children. First, *we can use the media as a means to train the child to deal with all parts of society.* Our attitude toward the technology should be neutral. Praise those programs that are wholesome and instructive; help the child evaluate those that are not. We want to train our children to use television to their best advantage. Similarly, we can rent movie videos that have worthwhile themes and use them as a springboard for discussing the right values—or wrong ones— portrayed by characters. And we can make the Internet a window to a wide world of information for our children, helping our children as we spot truth—and error—together.

Second, *we parents must do all in our power to prevent our children from being desensitized to the unhealthy messages and influences in society.* We do this by closely monitoring what they are exposed to. That includes movies they want to see and TV programs they watch.

I believe it is a mistake to forbid children from watching television or understanding other forms of media. One reason I believe this is that almost all American homes have television sets and children are naturally drawn to them. When we prohibit our children from viewing television in our homes, they will be drawn to watch programs in the homes of their friends. This will most assuredly develop in them an attitude that their home is missing something, is less appealing than other homes. When they reach those years of normal passive-aggressive behavior, they will be extremely prone to use television (in someone else's home or in yours) as an avenue to act out these passive-aggressive tendencies.

I realize that some parents have handled this problem by homeschooling or otherwise reducing a child's exposure to the media. This approach does help prevent the young child from being desensitized, but it does not train the child to cope with the ubiquitous TV set or the Internet or much of the music on the scene today. (See chapter 11 for guidelines on Internet use by your children.) A child needs protection from what is harmful and training in how to evaluate and provide self-protection when parents are not present.

If your children attend movies and other outside entertainment, you will want to have the same kinds of guidelines regarding number of hours as you do for television. Also, observe the movie ratings. Children should not see R-rated movies, if for no other reason than that doing so would be breaking the law. In addition, many PG-13 and PG movies are questionable. I recommend you read movie reviews in the local newspaper to know the popular movies and their themes and to help your children screen the candidates. You may conclude they shouldn't attend a particular PG-rated film. If so, be sure to give a reason. For instance, "There is nudity"; or, "It's obvious from the movie review that this has loads of profanity and violence, and I don't want you to get accustomed to such words and scenes." Talk with your children about why the movie is not acceptable. As they begin to go out with their peers for entertainment, you should know where they are going, who they will be with, and what they will be watching or doing.

Third, *we should offer healthy entertainment in our homes.* By healthy entertainment, I mean active forms that involve your child and either her siblings or her friends. I do not mean passive forms, such as watching TV, viewing videos, or playing video games. Especially as they become teenagers, we want our children to *want* to be home. So make your home the favorite place of your children as well as their friends.

When your children are home, you know what they are doing and that puts you in a positive position to interact and relate to them. When they are at a friend's house, you lose that advantage.

Have a variety of activities available for your children and their friends. And make yourself available to interact.

When our son David went to his high school reunion, he and the others were given a questionnaire asking about their memories from high school days. One question was about the favorite hangout. Our house was rated second after a local eating place. Our efforts really paid off. And, one of the best things was that we were able to get to know our children's friends well and feel close to most of them. We are still in touch with many of them.

Fourth, *we should make the television option less important in our homes.* The way to handle the problem of television is to have a set that is adequate—but barely so. It will be in color but can be rather small. Next, place it in a nonprominent area of the house, thus making it inconvenient to watch. And never put one in your bedroom. Remember, the best teacher is role-modeling. If you lie in bed watching television, you are setting a hazardous example.

Your child needs to see you watching TV for specific reasons on specific occasions, not as a routine part of every day. For example, you can obtain most of the news from newspapers rather than television. By doing this you are teaching your children to use television minimally and also to choose reading as a way of keeping up.

SUGGESTIONS FOR WISE USE OF TELEVISION

Television remains the pervasive entertainment medium in most homes. Assuming you have a TV set and it operates daily, here are suggestions for its proper use.

- Set time limits for viewing television. Some wise parents allow one-half hour a day. I recommend limiting TV viewing to between sixty and ninety minutes per day.

- Examine the TV viewing guide and determine what programs are suitable for children. From the list of suitable programs, let your children choose the ones they want to watch, within the time limits you have set.

- Prohibit TV viewing before school (it will slow down them and you) or after school until all homework is done.

- Keep the television off during meals.

- Stick with the schedule you have decided upon. Don't give in to making exceptions, just to keep the kids quiet or out of your hair.

- Avoid using television as a pacifier or a cheap baby-sitter.

- Find other forms of entertainment. You will need to be involved with your children until they are able to entertain themselves with means other than television, such as games, reading, CDs, and radio. This will take an effort on your part, but the rewards will be great.

- Have some good video movies or taped TV programs on hand for times when you need some instant family entertainment.

- Watch television with your children. During and after programs you can share your ideas and reactions. This will naturally lead into teaching situations, as you talk together about what is important or appropriate, what expresses the values of your family, what supports or opposes Christian beliefs, etc.

STAYING INVOLVED

If you have gotten into the habit of sharing media experiences with your child, you will find that she will ask more questions as she grows older. Some of these questions will be about forms of media that you do not think are appropriate for your family. When this day comes, if you have done a good job of nurturing, training, and protecting her, you may decide to let her watch the program in question—with you. Since you have protected her from being desensitized to this type of entertainment in the past, the new exposure will have the desired effect on her. She will be uncomfortable with it and probably repulsed.

You will also have the opportunity to talk with her about it and to share your feelings and thoughts. This kind of discussion will probably include ways to relate to her friends who have been desensitized to such entertainment and find no fault with it.

The many available media in the twenty-first century can be exciting and positive, if you use them that way. But you must be sure that unscrupulous people are not taking advantage of your children and teenagers. This means that you need to stay involved and know what is happening both in your home and in the wider world of television, the Internet, and the movies.

As David Walsh of the National Institute of Media and Family said, "The media are probably more powerful than we realize, and if parents are responsible for caring for their children, then our definition of *caring* has to keep pace with a changing media world."[13]

As parents we can keep up with the constant change by staying in communication with one another. We can also stay tuned to our children's viewing habits by participating in their television and computer lives. As we share experiences in this area, we will have a great avenue to remain close to our children as they grow.

NOTES

1. Nielsen media research, 1996, as reported in *The World Almanac and Book of Facts 1998* (Mahwah, N. J.: World Almanac, 1997) 259.

2. Peter H. Gibbon, "The End of Admiration: The Media and the Loss of Heroes," *Imprimis* (Hillsdale College), May 1999, 2.

3. Nielsen media research, *The World Almanac and Book of Facts 1998,* 260.

4. "Readers' Letters," *Good Housekeeping,* February 1998, 18.

5. Ibid.

6. Ibid.

7. Beenea A. Hyatt, "Man Charged in Solicitation of Teen Girl," *Chattanooga Times,* 2 May 1999, A16.

8. Ibid., 55.

9. Susan Roth, "Army Psychologist Cites Video Games," *Chattanooga Times,* 6 May 1999, A7.

10. The ratings are established by the Entertainment Software Ratings Board. For more information on the ratings system, see www.esrb.com. For the useful "ESRB Parent's Guide," see www.esrb.com/parent.html.

11. Mary Cagney, "Why Hollywood Doesn't Like You," *Christianity Today,* 10 August 1998, 64.

12. David Walsh, *Selling Out America's Children* (Minneapolis: Fairview, 1994), 28.

13. David Walsh, "Computer Violence: Are Your Kids at Risk?" *Reader's Digest,* January 1999, 4.

Chapter Eight

Training Your Child Spiritually

The most excellent end for which we are created is that one should teach another about God, what He is in His being, what His will is, how He is minded towards us.

MARTIN LUTHER

Pat and I sat on a front row of the church, watching our younger son, Dale, get married to Kisha. As I looked on, I was overwhelmed with praise to God. I remembered all the times Dale and I had spent sharing spiritual truths and the many opportunities I had to teach him about the goodness of God. I marveled at the maturity of both Dale and Kisha.

The Lord had given me many precious moments of helping Dale to grow in every way over the years and to develop a close relationship with the Lord. This meant so much to me when I saw Dale joining together with a wonderful woman in a genuine Christian marriage. *Father, how can I thank you enough?* I thought. *You are so good!*

As a Christian parent, you too desire for your children to follow in your faith, just as Pat and I did. You want them to confess Jesus Christ as their Lord and then mature in the meanings of that faith for all areas of life. For this to happen as a natural extension of the home, your children need to identify and relate closely with you and feel deeply loved and accepted.

"But I know people from less than happy homes who have become strong Christians," you may say, "some of them after long rebellion or anger against their parents." Yes, and we can thank God that His grace is not confined to the good behavior of parents, or many of us would be forever lost. But people who become believers in spite of their parents often struggle with long conflicts reaching back to events and attitudes from childhood. This is especially troubling if the home is ostensibly Christian but lacks any evidence of real trust in the Lord.

I know this internal conflict is not what you want for your children. For this reason, you need to continually ensure that the love bond in your family is strong. Without that, children will react to parental guidance, and especially spiritual guidance, with resentment and hostility.

WHERE SPIRITUAL TRAINING BEGINS

Emotionality and spirituality are not separate entities, but are related to and dependent on one another. Parents who want to guide a child spiritually will first care for him emotionally. This care begins when a child is born—and even before birth, in the sense of the mother's health and emotional stability. How well you nourish your child emotionally has the greatest overall effect on his welfare.

The Powerful Role of Our Experiences

A major part of your child's emotional development—and intellectual development—are experiences he undergoes, positive and negative. In fact, the greatest determinant in how the brain neurons of a child connect is what the child experiences. Your child was born with over 100 billion neurons (nerve cells) in her brain, roughly the number of stars in the Milky Way. According to medical research, not all of these neurons are connected or wired at birth. Over time, these neurons gradually become connected.

These neural networks form along the lines of experiences she is exposed to. This means that her environment, which is primarily controlled by you, determines the development and makeup of her brain. (Genetic factors also influence some of these connections.) We are not talking here about something intangible, but about the physical structure of your child's brain. Neurobiologist Carla Shatz of the University of California, Berkeley, states that at birth "what the brain has done is lay out circuits that are its best guess about what's required for vision, for language, for whatever." Your child's sensory experiences take this rough blueprint and progressively refine it.

During the first year of life, there is a phenomenal production of connections between the neurons. The brain also eliminates connections or synapses which are less used. When the child is about ten, the excess neurons are gradually eliminated, leaving behind a brain or mind whose patterns of emotion and thought are unique.[1]

If your child's brain is deprived of a stimulating environment, it suffers. Researchers at the Baylor College of Medicine in Houston found that children who don't play much or who are rarely touched develop brains 20 to 30 percent smaller than normal for their age. "By the age of three, a child who is neglected or abused bears marks that, if not indelible, are exceedingly difficult to erase."[2]

Neurobiologists now agree that a baby does not come into the world as a blank slate or as a genetically preprogrammed automaton. *His future depends largely on what he experiences and on how he is treated.* The first circuits the brain constructs are those that govern emotions. "Beginning around two months of age, the distress and contentment experienced by newborns start to evolve into more complex feelings of joy and sadness, envy, and empathy, pride and shame."[3] Loving care provides a baby's brain with the right kind of emotional stimulation. However, neglecting the child can produce brain-wave patterns which dampen happy feelings and can produce anxiety and abnormal stress responders.

Bruce Perry, a physician at the Baylor College of Medicine, argues that the role parents play in setting up the neural circuitry in large part determines how children regulate their response to stress. For example, children who are physically abused early in life develop brains that are exquisitely tuned to danger. At the slightest threat, their hearts race, their stress hormones surge and their brains anxiously track the nonverbal cues that might signal the next attack. Because the brain develops in sequence, with more primitive structures stabilizing their connections first, early abuse is particularly damaging.[4]

In his book *Emotional Intelligence,* Daniel Goleman writes about emotional memory and calls early experiences, such as abuse or emotional deprivation, "rough, wordless blueprints for emotional life." He adds:

> Since these earliest emotional memories are established at a time before infants have words for their experience, when these emotional memories are triggered in later life there is no matching set of articulated thoughts about the response that takes us over. One reason we can be so baffled by our emotional outbursts, then, is that they often date from a time early in our lives when things were bewildering and we did not yet have words for comprehending events. We may have the chaotic feelings, but not the words for the memories that formed them.[5]

The Early Adolescent Brain

The brain continues its rapid growth until about the age of ten. It is important for parents to realize that the child's brain is making its connections over many years. Otherwise they can too readily "fall into the trap of expecting children to have reached a maturity far beyond their years, forgetting that each emotion has its preprogrammed moment of appearance in a child's growth."[6] With the onset of puberty, the brain undergoes what Goleman calls "pruning," as "the brain actually loses the neuronal connections that are less used, and forms strong connections in those synaptic circuits that have been utilized the most. . . . Experience, particularly in childhood, sculpts the brain."[7]

Until the last decade of the twentieth century, many scientists believed that the brain was fully developed by puberty. I was never of this opinion, and in *How to Really Love Your Teenager* argued that teenagers are more children than adults. Now researchers have come to the same conclusion. A cover story in *U.S. News & World Report* reported that the neural circuitry of the brain is not all in place until the late teens or early twenties.

Indeed, the brain inside a teenager's skull is in some ways closer to a child's brain than to an adult's. Still being forged are the connections between neurons that affect not only emotional skills but also physical and mental abilities. . . . And these still-developing neural links leave a teenager vulnerable: Depression in adolescence may set up circuits in the brain that will make it much harder to treat the illness later in life.[8]

The pruning of the brain that begins about the age of twelve is "a sort of 'use it or lose it' system for ensuring that the brain nourishes only the neurons and synapses that are useful. . . . Until the prefrontal cortex has been pruned, most young teenagers don't yet have all the brain power they need to make good judgments."[9]

William Greenough of the University of Illinois says of that pruning time, "It is the overproduction of synaptic connections followed by their loss that leads to patterns in the brain. Potential for greatness may be encoded in the genes, but whether that potential is realized as a gift for mathematics, say, or a brilliant criminal mind, depends on patterns etched by experience in those critical early years."[10]

One of the final steps in making an adult brain is the coating of nerves in white matter, fatty cells that spiral around the shaft of nerves like vines around a tree. . . . Some of the nerves that become sheathed during adolescence connect areas of the brain that regulate emotions, judgment, and impulse control.[11]

How does this affect us as parents? The findings seem to be saying, "Start early. Be involved positively. Realize that patterns of feelings and emotions are developing during the child's early years and adolescence." We can have a hand in developing those patterns—patterns that will determine how healthy a child's emotional life and spiritual life will become. They can determine the overall emotional state—how the child perceives most areas of life; how positive or negative she is; how resilient she is; how well she can cope with stress. The pattern set early can affect her later in how well she will rebound from setbacks; how she will be motivated by fear, guilt, pressure—or a positive, liberating desire to do what is right. It determines how she feels and, therefore, how she behaves.

The findings about the brain's development are awesome. And, they confirm the overwhelming influence that parents have in their children's lives. They endorse the power of proactive, relational parenting. For Christians, there is no time for reactive parenting. Too much is at stake. We need to be proactive as we love and guide and train our children.

A FOUNDATION FOR SPIRITUAL MANAGEMENT

The Great Need for a Spiritual Base

By the teen years, children are learning to manage the behaviors and the patterns that are somewhat set in the brain. And by then they are able to evaluate the influences in their lives to that point. In a survey on teenagers done by the Barna Research Group, the overwhelming choice of influencer in their lives was their parents. On a question about who had bearing on their spiritual lives, six times as many teenagers credited parents as those who mentioned peers, and three times more mentioned parents than those who said the church was the primary influence.[12]

What a comfort and a wake-up call to parents. Our children's spiritual lives are in our hands, and this includes not only certain theological beliefs and practices but also their entire approach to morals and ethics.

While preparing this book manuscript, I saw a sad example of a young woman just out of her teens who suddenly appeared in the national spotlight. After the presidential impeachment hearings were completed, ABC-TV's Barbara Walters interviewed Monica Lewinsky, the woman who almost brought down a president. Miss Lewinsky, who had several sexual encounters with men before her liaison with the president, will remain a sad and telling example of what our degenerate culture can produce, if unhindered. My impression was that her concerns, goals, and motives have been destructive to herself and to those with whom she is involved.

In the interview, she seemed to have no sense of personal

identity, regarding herself primarily as a sexual object. She expressed no regard for the country or for the consequences of her behavior. In her desire to be attractive and acceptable, she made herself available to men. She also showed herself as being exquisitely vulnerable, especially to unscrupulous men who took advantage of her.

Lewinsky is an extreme example of what our culture unabated can do to our young people, yet children from any family can be touched in similar but lesser ways. It is imperative that we give our children something vital and strong that can act as a standard by which to manage the turmoil that they encounter in adolescence, as well as in the culture. To counteract what is surrounding our young people, we parents need to provide a foundation on which their lives can be based. This foundation must be something strong enough to last a lifetime and one that can be passed on to our grandchildren.

Such a foundation for life must give stability in times of unprecedented change, when those who hold to spiritual values are so often looked upon as hypocritical, judgmental, and self-righteous. Citizens no longer agree on high values and standards and saying something is wrong is to be labeled "intolerant." In a sensitive, "politically correct" society, our children are being taught that calling something "sin" is to be nonaccepting, mean-spirited, and narrow. We parents are made to feel that we should tolerate any behavior, attitude, or belief.

An Indispensable Treasure

In such a setting, it is not easy for parents to pass on their Christian faith and the moral and ethical standards that proceed from that faith. However, if our children are to stand for anything valuable, and to have guidelines to light their way, we must give them this most valuable treasure.

What is this indispensable treasure that gives purpose and meaning to life? This peace-giving possession, which provides life-sustaining direction and which satisfies the craving of every heart, is God Himself. He is intimately personal yet can be shared. He is strength in times of conflict and comfort in times of distress. He has provided help in the past and promises to be with us now and in the future, to give direction and guidance, and to be closer to us than a brother.

God the Father gives wisdom in confusion and correction when there is error. Our Lord will allow loss and pain, but He will always heal and replace the loss with something better. He will not force Himself on us but patiently waits to be accepted. He does not coerce us into doing His will, and is deeply distressed and hurt when we follow wrong paths.

In His Word, our Father offers us directions He wishes to be carried out, and He extends His promises to those who obey Him. He wants us to love Him because He first loved us, and yet He made us with free will so that we can accept or reject Him. He wants to take care of us, but refuses to force Himself upon us. His greatest desire is to be our loving Father, and yet He will not intrude. If we desire this loving and caring Father-child relationship with Him, we need first to accept His offer. He waits for us to open our lives to Him and become His children.

Such a personal and intimate relationship with God through His Son, Jesus Christ, is the most important factor in life. This is the ultimate foundation for goodness and meaning, and it is this that we must pass along to our children. We cannot decide for them, but we can train them so that they will come to a place of decision for themselves, and have enough sense of the goodness and love of God to desire this for themselves.

TEACHING SPIRITUAL VALUES

To guide your child spiritually, you need to keep two essentials in mind. The first is that you have a personal and vital relationship with God yourself. The second is that your child be assured of your unconditional love—the same love God has given you. With these essentials in place, your child will be ready to accept and incorporate spiritual values into her own life.

As you teach your child spiritual values, whether by living your faith before her or by instructing her verbally, you need to make the learning experience as pleasant as possible. A child is much more emotional than cognitive and, therefore, much more apt to remember feelings than facts. She will therefore be greatly influenced by the way she feels while being taught and will remember the emotions of a particular situation more than she will recall the details of a lesson.

When my two sons were ten and six, I took them fishing one summer in North Carolina. We were having such a good time that we decided to continue fishing after dark. It was a clear night, and soon the stars shone brightly. Even the Milky Way was easily visible. It was truly an awesome sight. In such a setting, our conversation led naturally to the wonder of it all.

My older son, Dave, said, "Dad, this makes me feel so small. I know our earth is just a dot in this whole universe."

"It shows the magnificence of God, David, just how great He really is. And yet He still cares about us on this little planet and looks after us every day. I'm so thankful that it was He who made this great universe, and that He is good and kind. That He loves us."

"Why is He good?" Dale asked.

"I don't know a lot of things, Dale. I don't know why God is good. But I do know that He is and that He loves us. I see this every day. Just being here with you boys tonight is one of His greatest gifts. Seeing you and David becoming fine, wonderful boys is proof to me that He loves us. He is constantly giving us gifts and blessings to show us that He loves us."

That fishing trip was a precious time with my wonderful boys. It made a deep impression on their hearts, as well as mine.

This principle about emotions and facts applies also to formal learning situations in a church setting, too. A child in a Sunday school class will remember exactly how he felt long after he forgets what was taught. This means that to some extent the emotional atmosphere is more important than the details of the lesson.

Creating a pleasant learning experience doesn't mean that a teacher (or parent) caters to a child's desire for amusement; but she will treat him with respect, kindness, and concern. A teacher must not criticize, humiliate, or otherwise put down a child. Because the content of a spiritual lesson is extremely important, it is crucial that the atmosphere be conducive to accepting the lesson. If the lesson at church or home is boring or degrading for a child, he is very likely to reject even the best teaching. This is particularly true when religious truths are involved. In a negative setting, a child can develop a bias against religious matters.

I have heard many times the following popular misconception: "I want my child to make up his own mind after being exposed to various ideas. He shouldn't have to believe what I do. I want him to learn about different religious philosophies so that he can make his own decision."

Parents who think this way are either copping out or are ignorant of the world we live in. They are conforming exactly with "political correctness," accepting everything and judging nothing. In this present culture, or in any culture, every child needs continual guidance and training and clarification in ethical, moral, and spiritual matters. Without this, he will become increasingly confused about his world and wonder if he can survive.

As Christians we do have solid answers to most of life's conflicts and seeming contradictions, but we know that it takes years to lead our children to the point where they can see these working on a daily basis. Unless we provide our children with this foundation of knowledge and understanding and guidance, they may later ask us, "What is life all about? What does it mean?"

Our culture has become a maze through which children try to find their way to safety. Without true guides and counselors, they will lose their way. It always amazes me that parents can spend thousands of dollars and go to great lengths to see that their children are well educated, and yet neglect the most important preparation of all—a readiness for life's spiritual and moral battles and a way to find true meaning. We must prepare our children spiritually. If we do not provide guidance for our children, others are standing ready to do so. But if we provide the spiritual guidance they crave, we and they will be the richer for it. Teaching our children the ways of God will later bless our home in ways we cannot imagine.

WAYS TO PREPARE
YOUR CHILDREN SPIRITUALLY

While organized religious instruction and activities in churches, Christian camps, and special youth clubs are extremely important to your developing child, nothing influences him more than his training at home. Parents cannot afford to leave spiritual training to other people. And yet you may be wondering what things are most important to pass along to your children. Let's look at a few.

Use Stories and Events

First, *talk about the meaning of stories and events.* Stories are a highly effective way of teaching your children, especially when you read a story and then talk about it in a relaxed and loving way. Bedtime is one of the best times in a child's day, since you then have no competition from other activities. Also, most children want to delay bedtime, and you can take advantage of this desire to spend valuable time with them. In this warm atmosphere, you can meet their emotional needs and also give them spiritual training and guidance.

It is fairly simple to give your child basic scriptural facts, such as the names and actions of Bible characters. But ultimately, that is not what you are after. Your child needs to understand what meaning biblical characters and principles have for him personally. You should teach this with passion and commitment. When you guide a child spiritually, you are combining all the elements of unconditional love—eye contact, focused attention, touch, as well as a deep sharing of the best you have to offer your child.

Talk About Your Own Experiences

Second, *share your own experiences with your children.* With the factual knowledge gained from church, Sunday school, and home, children have only the raw materials with which to grow spiritually. They need to learn to use this knowledge effectively and accurately to become spiritually mature. To do this, they need the experience of walking with God daily and learning to trust Him personally.

They will have an interest in *your* experiences with God, so share your own spiritual life with them. Of course, your response depends on the quality of what you have to share. How much you share depends on your children's level of development, age, and ability to comprehend. As your children mature, you will want to gradually increase talking with them about how you love God, walk daily with Him, rely on Him and seek His guidance and help, and thank Him for His love, care, gifts, and answered prayer.

Look for opportunities to reveal to each child events showing God in action *as they happen,* rather than afterward. What you share with your children will depend on their ages and maturity, since you don't want them to feel anxious about finances or insecure about where they live. If as parents you demonstrate a strong confidence in the loving guidance of your heavenly Father, your children will see and feel more than you can express to them in words. As it is appropriate, invite your children to join you in prayer. That way they will be part of the experience of coming to God in prayer and also of expecting that the answers will come.

As you do this over many years, your children will be building memories of God working in the life of their family. Also, they will learn to go to the Lord with their own concerns. There is so much truth in the old saying, "Experience is the best teacher." Let your child share in yours and learn alongside you to trust God more.

A child needs to learn how the Lord meets personal and family needs, including the financial. For example, she should know when you are praying for the needs of others; or when you are asking God for solutions to problems, as appropriate to the child's age. And don't forget to keep her informed about how God is working in your life, or how He is using you to minister to others. Of course, your child should certainly know that you are praying for her individual and particular needs.

Demonstrate Forgiveness

Finally, *model forgiveness.* You teach by example how to forgive and how to find forgiveness from God and other people. You do this first by forgiving and by asking for forgiveness—of your spouse or even your child—when you make a mistake.

Yes, if you wrong your child, you should ask for your child's forgiveness. I cannot overemphasize how important this is. At the point when you are angry and don't feel like asking for forgiveness from your child, try to remember this truth: *True intimacy comes from resolved conflict.* You can even come to regard conflict as an opportunity to draw closer to one another—if you manage your own anger and can lead family members to a loving resolution of the problem.

Forgiveness remains a crucial matter within families. So many people today have problems with guilt and cannot forgive or feel forgiven. Those who have learned how to forgive those who offend, and who are able to ask for and receive forgiveness, demonstrate one mark of mental and emotional health and live with greater peace than those who cannot.

GIVE YOUR CHILDREN OPTIMISM AND HOPE

Giving Optimism

As your children grow into adolescence, they need optimism and hope. In a time of decayed values, adults who are willing and able to uplift their children's hearts provide much comfort.

You are in the best position to give this precious gift, but it takes work. You shouldn't listen to the proclaimers of gloom and doom or pass along their message. Teenagers are so sensitive to pessimism, especially from their parents. You do not have to buy into the despair of others—you can have faith in God and also in yourself. Encourage your children in their progress. Tell them of their great potential and of God's great plans for them. *Encourage* means to "inspire courage"; your words will give them courage to face the future.

God is the author of hope, and He gives us hope. I suggest that you regularly read chapter 11 of the book of Hebrews, where you're reminded of a hope that cannot be destroyed. Remember that the wonderful promises of God are true and that God Himself is faithful and constant in His love and care for us. In the Bible we have so many promises that offer us hope. Consider just these four:

> And we know that in all things God works for the good of those who love him, who have been called according to his purpose. (Romans 8:28)

"For I know the plans I have for you," declares the Lord, "plans to prosper you and not to harm you, plans to give you hope and a future." (Jeremiah 29:11)

"Do not fear, for I am with you; do not be dismayed, for I am your God. I will strengthen you and help you; I will uphold you with my righteous right hand." (Isaiah 41:10)

A righteous man may have many troubles, but the Lord delivers him from them all. (Psalm 34:19)

My former pastor, Moncrief Jordan, told me about Bart, whom he visited regularly. Bart had many physical ailments and eventually both of his legs had to be amputated. Pastor Jordan thought that this would surely break his joyful and optimistic view of life, but it didn't. Bart would still swing himself with a trapeze device from his bed to a wheelchair and roll himself down to the parlor in the nursing home where he lived. There he would play the piano and sing until he had many others singing with him. During his last years, he was the channel of hope and joy to many people.

Giving an Enduring Hope

Christian parents, of all adults, can offer their children a hope in God that endures the pessimism and live-for-the-moment attitude of much of teen culture. Never was this more clear than in the responses of many of the surviving teenagers in April 1999 following the massacre at Columbine High School in Littleton, Colorado. Two high school students shot more than a dozen fellow students. Afterward, twelve students and one teacher were dead or dying, and the two shooters had taken their own lives. Fifteen people died. It made no sense.

After the deaths, more than one hundred grief counselors were available to help the Columbine survivors deal with their pain. As it turned out, those counselors didn't have many young people to talk to, because the teenagers and their families chose another place for comfort and guidance—their churches.

Charles Colson quoted one pastor in the area as saying, "Kids aren't wanting psychology at this time. . . . They want to know, 'Why did this happen?'" He pointed out that the "grief work" model is based on Freud's "work of mourning," which rules out life after death. Thus, it does not encourage hope or give spiritual answers to tragedy. Often, "grief work" includes venting negative emotions. [13]

Most of the kids of Columbine High School knew that this wasn't what they needed, and they went to their pastors and priests for help. They wanted the hope that only Christ can give, Colson noted.

One of the shooting victims was Cassie Bernall. When one of the gunmen pointed his weapon at her and asked, "Do you believe in God?" she answered, "Yes, I believe in God." He then took her life with a blast of the gun. On the night of her murder, Cassie's brother found a journal entry she had just written. It included the words from Philippians 3:10–11 [TLB] that Cassie had made her own:

> Now I have given up on everything else—I have found it to be the only way to really know Christ and to experience the mighty power that brought Him back to life again, and to find out what it means to suffer and to die with Him. So, whatever it takes, I will be one who lives in the fresh newness of life of those who are alive from the dead.

Hope for the Future Generation

During the same week as the tragedy at Columbine, 73,000 young people gathered in Pontiac, Michigan, to proclaim their optimism about the future and to resist the attitudes of many of their peers. In a huge football stadium where the Detroit Lions play, the teenagers met, according to one reporter, "to declare they would live with honor, take responsibility for their actions, and respect authority." The gathering, named Teen Mania Day One, centered around the crucial question, "What kind of Christianity will we take into the next millennium?" The teenagers read in unison and then signed a Teenage Bill of Rights that included vows to abstain from premarital sex, illegal drugs, and alcohol.[14]

In a recent interview, Billy Graham expressed his optimism about many of today's teenagers and said that he spends as much time as he can in focused ministry to this upcoming generation, because he feels that they are seeking to know God in this time of turmoil and mixed values.

Yes, there is hope for our teenagers and younger children. It is so important that they come to understand and deeply believe that Christian hope does not depend on what the world does to them. It depends only on what they do in the world as they live in response to God's great love for us. As parents we can be encouragers, dispensers of the hope that our children and teenagers so desperately need—even in the best of times and certainly in the worst.

NOTES

1. J. Madeleine Nash, "Fertile Minds," *Time* Special Report, 3 February 1997, 49.

2. Ibid., 51.

3. Ibid., 53.

4. Ibid., 55.

5. Daniel Goleman, *Emotional Intelligence* (New York: Bantam, 1995), 22.

6. Ibid., 274.

7. Ibid., 224.

8. Shannon Brownlee, "Inside the Teen Brain," *U.S. News & World Report,* 9 August 1999, 46–47.

9. Ibid., 48.

10. Nash, "Fertile Minds," *Time,* 56.

11. Brownlee, "Inside the Teen Brain," *U.S. News,* 53.

12. "The Barna Report," quarterly newsletter of the Barna Research Group (Ventura, Calif.), January–March 1999, 8.

13. Charles Colson, "Good Grief—Faith Versus Freud," BreakPoint commentary radio broadcast, 13 May 1999.

14. Josh Kennedy, "73,000 Teens Pledge Responsibility," *Christianity Today,* 14 June 1999, 13.

Chapter Nine

Fear, Anxiety, and Depression

For God did not give us a spirit of timidity, but a spirit of power, of love and of self-discipline.

2 TIMOTHY 1:7

Fear is strangling our society on several levels, to such an extent that many people do not realize how much their lives are controlled by it. Very naturally, parents are affected by this generalized fear, as well as by very specific anxieties that have to do with their own children. Unfortunately, these feelings build on one another, causing some parents to behave in illogical and harmful ways toward their children.

FOUR FEARS

Most parents face four fears. Let's look at these progressive fears:

- Fear of what is going to happen to our child in this threatening culture

- Fear of our child's behavior and anxiety about disciplining him

- Fear of the child himself

- Fear of teenagers in general

Fear of the Future

Never before has the American society posed such threatening problems to children and teenagers. In earlier times children were more under the control of their own nuclear and extended family. Today many young parents feel that they are losing control to unseen forces that can harm their children. Naturally they are afraid. They have no experience in parenting and are trying to make their way through a confusing maze, trying to win at a game in which the odds seem to be against them. They want to do the best by their children, but fear that they will not.

If you fall into that "younger parent" category, either by your age or the age of your little children, consider tapping the shoulders of older and more experienced parents for help. Those who have raised their own children to be responsible and happy adults understand what younger parents need to know and do to assure that their children will do well. Most are able and willing to point to paths which will help you provide your children everything they need to prosper, and also to alert you to traps and pitfalls to avoid. You know that you can't afford to make critical mistakes—you need to do it right the first time. In our threatening culture, there are few second chances.

Fear of Child's Behavior, Leading to Permissiveness and Authoritarianism

Parents have other fears in rearing their children, but one of the most undermining is the fear of the child's behavior and of disciplining him. As a result, the parents often let the child rule the roost. Many parents today seem to want their children to lead the way. Naturally, these parents are not in control of their homes. If a child is strong-minded and enjoys defying authority, control and discipline become a daily nightmare. As the child takes control, he becomes increasingly headstrong and parents feel even more bewildered.

In their fear, many parents become permissive. The child's

behavior further deteriorates as he continually (though indirectly) asks that critical question, "Do you love me?" through his misbehavior. He is waiting for the parents to correct him, to show that they care and are involved. At this point the war seems lost, because nothing works with a child whose emotional tank is empty.

In their frustration, these permissive parents then resort to punishment administered with anger and resentment. They are in the punishment trap, because the more they use angry punishment, the more resentful and defiant their unloved child will be. The child can then manipulate his parents and they, in turn, become increasingly frustrated and tyrannical; or, they may give up in despair. Either way, they become permissive. Parenting based on fear is crippling and results in misery for all.

Other parents respond to their fears by being rigidly authoritarian. Determined to firmly and inflexibly control their child, they become overly concerned with discipline as a way to control their child's behavior. They assume that strong discipline (punishment) is the key to raising a well-behaved child. Their fear results in reactive parenting, and we have already shown the hazards of using this approach. Parents who use this method put the cart before the horse. To focus on discipline without taking the child's needs into account first will cause both parents and child to suffer. Reactive parenting always results in the overuse of corporal punishment, and a child living in the atmosphere of the punishment trap cannot grow to be her best.

Whenever we fear the child's role, we affect her perceptions. The child detects the fear and rigidity in her parents. She may perceive affection at times, but she knows it's based only on the conditional love of obeying her parents; she lacks the unconditional love she so desperately needs to grow and thrive. The overemphasis on discipline (punishment) cripples the parents' ability to nurture and train their child.

The first response to fear is a paralysis, and it causes parents to be too permissive. The second response is reactive parenting, and this puts too much emphasis on rigid discipline in an autocratic atmosphere. There is no need to follow either extreme. In order to produce a well-balanced child (and eventually an adult), a wise parent will employ proactive parenting, emphasizing what the child needs first. And the first need of every child is to be loved and to feel loved.

Fear of Our Child

The fear of our child's behavior and our anxiety about disciplining him leads to a fear of the child himself. We are no longer sure how to discipline and to respond. The child is different from us, and for those of us with more than one child, each child is different from the other. We want to do the right job with each, yet each seems to respond differently (part of their differing personalities, of course, as well as the degree they feel loved). We sometimes tell ourselves, *I don't understand my kid, and who knows what he will do next.*

Our Fears of Adolescents in General

We see this troubling phenomenon everywhere, especially in public places, such as malls. So many people (and some parents) look on teenagers as insensitive, uncaring, disrespectful troublemakers. The truth, however, is that the vast majority of teenagers today are wonderful, wholesome kids. Yes, some of them look pretty weird, showing their normal adolescent passive-aggression with skin-piercing rings and colored hair and other adornments. Yes, many are having unprecedented problems, but often these expressions reveal the deeper desires of their lives, what they are missing yet yearn for—unconditional love. They want an unconditional love that is active and caring enough to provide them with training and guidance.

Ours is not the first generation of teenagers to strike fear in adult hearts by their provoking uniqueness. Remember the youth of the sixties and seventies with their long hair, peace signs, sandals, and strange way of speaking? Of course, they had their own music, just as teens do today, which seems to have but one purpose—to drive parents out of their minds.

Yes, some of the ways teens have today of being different are inappropriate and unwholesome. The extremes and dangers which some of their forms of passive-aggressive behavior have taken are drugs, gross musical lyrics, sexual promiscuity, and more. These behaviors are fearful as well as dangerous for the young people.

A report published by Search Institute, a nonprofit research organization, concluded, "Americans are convinced that today's adolescents face a crisis—not in their economic or physical well-being but in their values and morals. Most Americans look at today's teenagers with misgiving and trepidation, viewing them as undisciplined, disrespectful and unfriendly."[1]

One reason so many adults perceive teens as disrespectful, rude, uncivil, and even dangerous is the media treatment of adolescents in movies and magazines. These alarming images make us forget the good indications of uniqueness in so many members of this up-and-coming generation. Teenagers today are significant persons who need our love and support as no other generation has. The ultimate solution as we enter the new century is the same as it was for the children growing up in the sixties: lots of unconditional love and acceptance of the person.

Americans are quite ambivalent about their teenagers. They are confused by them, on the one hand, but they have not given up on them, on the other. Americans care very deeply about their youth. I believe that we are seeing many signs of developing maturity in our young people. You will find more on this in *Parenting Your Adult Child,* a book I wrote with Gary Chapman.[2]

OVERCOMING THOSE FEARS

Some people, including parents, value childhood innocence over normal adolescent awakenings. This astonishes me. It's as though these adults assume or hope that children will never become teenagers. Most parents pursue reactive parenting with their younger children and then wonder why they have so many problems with them when they reach adolescence. The solution can only be to adopt a relational, proactive approach.

Fear is an awesome force that can distort your thinking and cause you to place the wrong emphasis in your parenting. Since it can cause you to be too permissive or too harsh, you need to overcome your fear and live above it, especially for the sake of your children. The best way to do this is to relate to your children in a positive, proactive way, giving them the nurture, training, and protection they need at every stage of their development. When you care for your children in this way, you can relax and know that you are being the best kind of parent. When you relax with your children, you can genuinely enjoy them, and in this kind of environment they will prosper.

The best environment for a child is a home where the parents are relaxed, where the atmosphere is laid-back, upbeat, restful, peaceful, and loving, with a good dose of humor thrown in. In such a home parents feel good about their parenting and are confident that their children are experiencing the best of care. And they can be confident that their parenting is unlikely to create future hang-ups for their children. As you take the time and effort to be proactive with your children, giving them what they need most, you will not need to fear for their future.

ANXIETY AND CARING HEARTS

Anxiety is a first cousin to fear and, like fear and anger, it is a feeling. The peculiar thing about anxiety is that it has both a good and a bad side. On the negative side, anxiety is worry or uneasiness about the future. On the positive side, anxiety is concern for something or someone. We all have a certain level of anxiety, some of us too much and some too little.

A person with too much anxiety is hampered in many areas. He is almost always self-conscious and has poor self-esteem. He finds it difficult to come across to others as competent, balanced, and self-assured. At the same time, he may be a deeply caring person, depending on how much negative or positive anxiety he possesses. If he has too much negative anxiety or worry about the future, he feels discomfort. If he has great amounts of positive anxiety, he will have a caring heart for others. The two usually go together.

While it is miserable to be anxiety-ridden, it is far worse not to feel any anxiety. People who lack anxiety have no compassion. In fact, part of the definition of sociopathic behavior is the lack of anxiety. Such people know the difference between right and wrong, but they don't care. They are able to focus on their own selfish ends without being concerned about the welfare of others. You can see that anxiety is a mix of blessing and curse. References in the Bible to anxiety mean the negative side. The following are two of the best known passages about negative worry:

"Therefore I tell you, do not worry about your life, what you will eat or drink; or about your body, what you will wear. . . . But seek first his kingdom and his righteousness, and all these things will be given to you as well. Therefore do not worry about tomorrow, for tomorrow will worry about itself." (Matthew 6:25, 33–34)

Do not be anxious about anything, but in everything, by prayer and petition, with thanksgiving, present your requests to God. And the peace of God, which transcends all understanding, will guard your hearts and your minds in Christ Jesus. (Philippians 4:6–7)

A HEALTHY BALANCE

Clearly as parents, we need balance. But so do our children. As parents, you want your children to be as free as possible from negative anxiety, and yet you also want them to be sensitive and caring persons. It is so rare to find a healthy balance—a caring and compassionate person who is not overcome with worry and fear. This lack of balance is one factor in the deterioration of our society. As people become increasingly anxious about the cares of life, they seem to have less regard for others. Also, normally compassionate people can feel nearly anesthetized to the troubles of life because they see and hear so much about tragedies so remote that they can do nothing to help.

How can we ensure that our children will be balanced persons who have control over worry and yet are caring people? The solution is to meet their emotional needs first, and then train them in loving ways in which discipline is an extension of that love.

If a child doesn't experience unconditional love, she will fail to develop positive anxiety, that is, a caring heart. If she experiences harsh punishment without first having her emotional tank filled, she will tend to develop negative anxiety, that is, a worrying spirit and an uneasiness about life, and especially about the future. A strong-willed and hardheaded child who is exposed to too little love and too much punishment, or both, will tend to suppress *all* anxiety and will likely develop sociopathic traits.

The only way to assure your child of a healthy balance of

anxiety is to give her what she needs. Be proactive in your parenting. To take the best care of your child, be sure you put the horse properly before the cart: Give unconditional love before everything else.

DEPRESSION IN OUR CHILDREN

Depression afflicts many children today. Fifteen years ago, it seemed quite rare, partly because it was seldom identified as such. However, we have seen an alarming rise in incidence in recent years. In 1998, psychologist Ronald Kessler of Harvard Medical School studied more than eight thousand Americans between the ages of fifteen and fifty-four. He found that only 2 percent of those now forty-five to fifty-four reported symptoms of clinical depression by their late teens. Among those now fifteen to twenty-four, 23 percent had serious depression before age twenty.[3] Today depression is hitting at ever younger ages, but we see no similar increase in other mental problems in this generation.

Consequences and Causes of Depression

One frightening aspect of these increasing problems with depression and anxiety in children is what they can lead to. New studies show that youngsters who develop depression or anxiety are three to four times more likely than their peers to have drug or alcohol abuse problems by their midtwenties, according to Yale Medical School epidemiologist Kathleen Meridangas.[4] And depression can lead to suicide. Significantly, suicide rates for American children and teens quadrupled between 1950 and 1995.

Nearly two-thirds of depressed people have had at least one other mental problem first, usually anxiety. Almost all children who are depressed are anxiety-driven. Studies show that children are finding this world to be a scarier place than it was for us when we were young. Depression is shared among kids from affluent or impoverished homes. Children from all backgrounds are experiencing symptoms of serious depression at a higher rate than any other generation in modern history.[5]

Greater physical isolation is also causing larger numbers of children to suffer depression. "Kids used to grow up in large, close-knit, extended families. And more grandparents sat in com-

forting, spiritual furniture. Children are alone more now," concluded psychologist Martin Seligman. "Individualism is rampant, and
it's not a good buffer against the defeats we all face."[6]

Depressed children differ from their peers in some significant ways:

- Their parents are more likely to be divorced or have
  much conflict in the home.

- Seriously depressed teens are seen by themselves and
  by teachers as socially less adept than their peers. According to University of Texas psychologist Kevin Stark,
  "They misread neutral scenarios as rejection and that
  tends to make them shy and withdrawn."[7]

- Depressed children are more likely to believe their bad
  experiences are caused by something permanently
  flawed in themselves, rather than by changeable behaviors or conditions.

- In teenagers we see a strong link between stress and depression.

Depression in Boys and in Girls

Depression is rarely discovered in boys, even those who
are deeply depressed. In his book *Real Boys: Rescuing Our Sons
from the Myths of Boyhood,* William Pollack of McLean
Hospital/Harvard Medical School states that depression is seriously underdiagnosed in boys.[8]

When a teenager has been moderately to severely depressed and feels he can endure it no longer, he will take action in
an attempt to alleviate his misery and distress. The behavior resulting from this depression is termed "acting out his depression."
There are many ways a teenager can act out his depression.

Boys tend to be more violent than girls. They may attempt
to relieve their depressive symptoms by stealing, lying, fighting,
driving too fast, or in criminal behavior, such as shooting others.
These behaviors are seldom recognized or even considered as
symptoms of depression. This is one of the main reasons depression is underdiagnosed in boys.

For girls, depression becomes much more common after the age of eleven, and during the next four years its incidence rises rapidly. By age eighteen, girls have twice the rate of depression as boys. Studies have shown that girls, like women, tend to dwell on problems more than males do. This means that more women than men experience depression in adulthood.

In her acclaimed book, *Reviving Ophelia,* Mary Pipher gives excellent insights as to why early adolescent girls are having such a difficult time. I highly recommend this book for all parents, and especially those who have daughters. Girls worry more than boys do, particularly about matters over which they have little or no control. Their subjects for worry include such things as appearance, family problems, weight, and popularity.

One cause of their worry is that they have been trained to please and to care for others.[9] Their dilemma is an important example of the negative and positive sides of anxiety. It generally occurs in persons who have caring hearts and also a great deal of uneasiness about themselves and their circumstances, including the future.

Difficulties in Identifying Depression

Because depression causes so many other problems that can mask it, the depression itself can be very difficult to identify. However, it is being identified with more frequency today than it was years ago, resulting in a greater use today of antidepressants.

Childhood depression is very subtle and tends to develop gradually and slowly. Because of its many causes and effects, it is also very complex. When a child develops a problem in school work, depression is usually the last cause to be considered. This is especially frustrating when the child's problem is caused by one factor but aggravated by depression. This makes treatment of the initial cause nearly impossible until the depression is first taken care of.

For instance, the child may have academic problems caused by a neurological difficulty but greatly aggravated by depression. After all academic interventions have been tried and failed, the depression is occasionally discovered and treated, but not often. When it is alleviated, the academic problem then becomes treatable.

Childhood depression is hard to identify because its symptoms are usually different from those of adults. Children may show typical adult symptoms such as long-term sadness and irritability, but because they are usually unable to express their feelings, their depression is often mistaken for normal childhood behavior.

Frequently an anxious parent will call to tell me that her daughter (or son) is behaving normally, looks all right, but somehow is not her old self. She seems distressed at times for no apparent reason. Not long ago, a caring mother called to tell me about her eleven-year-old daughter who seemed to be doing well most of the time. However, now and then she would say something like, "Whenever I watch the news, I feel that things are getting so bad. Sometimes I wonder if it is worth it to go on." This girl was found to be moderately depressed. After a short course of a mild antidepressant and some counseling, she had gained a new outlook on her life.

Keep in mind that depression can occur in any child, even in those who seem to have an ideal situation. This is especially true for sensitive children, who sense the many depressing influences in our world. And through the nightly news and entertainment programs, television brings most of these to our children's attention. Wise parents will protect children as much as possible from being bombarded with this depressing material. Every child needs to be exposed to heartening and uplifting influences as much as possible.

RECOGNIZING AND TREATING DEPRESSION

Symptoms of Depression

All parents need to understand childhood depression, since it can affect a child's development in so many ways. We have indicated the difficulties in identifying depression in children; yet there are many signs that can suggest depression in a child. Often the first manifestation of the depression is academic difficulties. This is because most symptoms of depression affect school performance.

Here are many of those symptoms. When a child displays several of these symptoms, depression is possible.

1. *Shortened attention span.* Depression can easily be mistaken for attention deficit disorder (ADD). Also, most children with ADD or ADHD (attention deficit hyperactive disorder) are depressed. Therefore, depression can mimic ADD/ADHD or may aggravate it. In most cases of ADD/ADHD, depression must be treated along with the other factors of the disorder. However, depression itself can cause severe academic problems.
2. *Decreased concentration.* The distractible child is unable to keep his mind on the task at hand. This sets him up for the next symptom.
3. *Daydreaming.* The child's mind tends to wander and retreat into fantasies, causing him to become even more distractible.
4. *Boredom.* As the child increasingly daydreams, he has difficulty paying attention and gradually loses interest in things he previously enjoyed.
5. *Decreased energy.* Parents too often assume that this is caused by too little sleep, too much activity, or a mild physical illness. However, depression can distract and drain a child's energy level and interest in interacting with others.
6. *Misbehavior.* This symptom is usually associated with every possible cause except depression. Regardless of the underlying cause, depression can easily aggravate misbehavior. For example, bad behavior caused by an empty emotional tank will naturally be worsened by the resulting depression. Some typical examples of misbehavior due to depression are disruption in school, aggression with peers, and regressive behavior, such as bedwetting or baby talk.
7. *Long-term sadness,* beyond normal reaction to bad news or disturbing events. Strangely, this symptom is frequently absent, even in the midst of depression.
8. *Anger.* You may be surprised to learn that depression causes anger. And it can aggravate an already existing problem with anger. Any time a child has difficulty with anger, depression should be considered as a cause.

9. *Anxiety.* When a child is anxiety ridden, depression should be investigated as a possible cause. While anxiety can make a child vulnerable to depression, the depression also causes anxiety. For people of all ages, there is a strong anxiety-depression link.
10. *Withdrawal.* The child does not interact with others, including school friends. He seems to be moving toward isolation.

Treatment of Depression and Managed Care

Managed care now dominates American health care. It has become popular for families primarily because of its cost-savings. However, managed care has made it more difficult for parents to have a child evaluated for psychological problems. Even in the face of known and serious mental illness, it is extremely difficult to get enough cooperation from an insurance company to even pay for a psychological or psychiatric evaluation. But proceeding to treatment before such an evaluation is like asking a surgeon to operate without first obtaining X rays. The result has been an overuse or wrong use of medications.

Formerly, pediatricians were able to have a child evaluated to ascertain if the child truly suffered from attention deficit hyperactive disorder and if a psychostimulant medication was actually indicated. Now, lacking this evaluation, many pediatricians are prescribing such medications because mothers or teachers have said the word "hyperactive."

This same problem exists with the detection and treatment of childhood depression. How is a pediatrician to know the true mental status of a child without a legitimate evaluation? As a result, childhood depression is seldom suspected; if it is, an antidepressant is prescribed without proper indications or follow-up. In the past several years, we have lost almost everything many dedicated people have brought to the mental health profession in this country. Thanks to managed care, there is essentially no mental health system left, especially for children.

The failure of managed care has also affected what should be a very important day in the life of a child—the first day of first grade. If a child has psychological or potential academic problems that are not corrected or compensated for before the first grade, that child will have difficulties for years to come. Before the decline of mental health care, we earnestly recommended that every child have a complete psychological and academic exam prior to entering first grade. This way we were able to identify almost any potential problem that child might have and either correct it or make sure that it would be handled appropriately. When such problems go undetected, they will most assuredly end in tragic results for the child and the parents.

While I still strongly recommend a complete evaluation for every child, I know the difficulties so many parents will encounter. Because most insurance companies will not pay for this, and because competent child psychiatrists and child psychologists are consequently having a hard time providing for their own families, the art of psychological/academic evaluations for children is fast disappearing. The best I can suggest is to try to find one of those rapidly disappearing evaluators who will give your child such an evaluation, even if you have to pay for it yourself. The most important advantage of this is that you will be able to plan for your child's educational future. And, if any tendencies to problems are found, you will know what they are and be able to take care of them.

To parents who find it impossible to obtain such an evaluation, I am going to say something I never dreamed I would say, much less write. However, with the health-care restrictions noted above, I feel that I have no choice. Do not be afraid to give your child an antidepressant such as Prozac or a psychostimulant such as Ritalin, if your pediatrician, noting several symptoms, prescribes it. I would rather see a child who does not really need these medicines taking them than a child who needs them being deprived of them.

This is not as drastic as it may sound, since the medications are relatively safe and with few side effects. I have never seen Ritalin or any SSRI (serotonin specific reuptake inhibitor) antidepressant harm a child; but I have seen countless children permanently harmed by being deprived of these medications when they needed them.

YOUR CRUCIAL ROLE

Whether you are dealing with fear, anxiety, or possible depression, you need to keep in mind that you have the greatest influence on your children, at any age. We know that depressed children are more likely than their peers to have parents who are guilt-inducing, controlling, rejecting, or disinterested. These are the very attitudes and behaviors that you want to avoid.

It is crucial to keep your children's emotional tanks full, giving them the training and protection they so greatly need, and then knowing when and how to release them to greater independence, little by little. No matter what others tell you, remember that you are the primary influence in your children's lives and that you are in the driver's seat when it comes to making decisions about their lives. You have the power and responsibility to safeguard your children from the negative and unwholesome influences of society and to give them what they most deeply need. No one else has the lifelong power to provide them with a foundation for a happy and meaningful life.

NOTES

1. Kathleen Kimball-Baker and Eugene Roehikepartain, "Are Americans Afraid of Teens?" *Assets,* newsletter of the Search Institute, Summer 1998, 7.
2. Ross Campbell and Gary Chapman, *Parenting Your Adult Child* (Chicago: Northfield, 1999), especially 17–21.
3. Marilyn Elias, "Childhood Depression," *USA Today,* 13 August 1998, 2D.
4. Ibid.
5. Ibid.
6. Ibid. Seligman is president of the American Psychological Association.
7. Ibid.
8. William Pollack, *Real Boys* (New York: Random House, 1998), 9.
9. Elias, "Childhood Depression," *USA Today,* 2D.

Chapter Ten

Motivating Your Child

Teach us, O Lord, to do little things as though they were great, because of the majesty of Christ who does them in us and who lives our life; and to do the greatest things as though they were little and easy, because of His omnipotence.

BLAISE PASCAL

A question parents frequently ask me is, "How do I motivate my child?" They are asking the right question, since motivation is one of the greatest factors determining how well a child progresses.

While we might hope that our children will be self-motivated, able to carry through on responsibilities with little or no prompting from us, we know that this probably won't be the case. On the other hand, we hope we won't have children who drive everyone crazy with an endless string of excuses and unfulfilled promises and assignments.

Most children fall somewhere between these two extremes, and tend to be more motivated in certain areas than in others. Their personal level of motivation has something to do with their natural aptitudes and also with their personal attitudes. It may be affected by their degree of good health and energy and is certainly influenced by the way they are raised.

Motivation is a complex subject, one which parents will do

well to try to understand. For it is not just the matter of your children being motivated, but also *how* they are motivated—in healthy or unhealthy ways. All children are motivated, but we want them to be stimulated by the right things in the right ways.

MOTIVATION 101

Discovering how to motivate your children is not something you learn in a crash course. You first need to understand how children are naturally motivated and what influence you as parents can have on motivating them correctly.

Conscious and Subconscious Motivations

Let's begin with the fact that we all have *conscious motivation* and *subconscious motivation*. We see in our children positive motivations in their desire to be pleasant and considerate of others. Such motivations come from good parenting in which the children have developed a healthy self-esteem and self-awareness, as well as love and respect for others. We may observe negative subconscious motivation when a child desires to upset others, especially authority figures, by refusing to do what is rightly expected. This is passive-aggressive behavior.

There is a great deal of misunderstanding regarding our motivations; most people have the idea that how their life turns out is determined by rational, thought-out, conscious decisions. How I wish that were true! The truth is that the course a person's life takes, and the decisions that he makes, are largely determined by subconscious motivations that are below the surface of his awareness. Since he is not aware of these motivations, he naturally assumes that he is using rational thought processes in determining his future. Until . . . until the day he wakes up, deeply confused, and wonders how he got to where he is now. He traces the events of the past years and tries to figure out how they have come about as they have.

Some subconscious motivations are genetically influenced by character traits—such as shyness or gregariousness. However, most subconscious motivations are determined by experiences in early life. And parents have the greatest influence on subconscious motivations. These subconscious motivations become strong influences on the way we feel and think. Therefore, they can essentially determine our decisions, especially our major life decisions, such as where we will live, whom we will marry, the work we go into, and the friends and activities in which we engage.

We all have some subconscious motivations. Some are good ones and some negative. Of course, the more positive subconscious motivations we have and the fewer negative ones, the better, for then we will have more control of our lives. And we will want to give our children positive motivations, including positive subconscious motivations.

Desires and Attitudes

As we consider how a child is motivated, we know that parents play a major role in the process. The most powerful motivator is a child's desire. When a child desires to do or have something, she is motivated. This is good if what she wants is appropriate. Naturally, her parents want her desires to be as positive as possible. But if her desire is to do or be what is inappropriate, her parents must teach her to do the right thing, in spite of her feelings.

Have you noticed how much motivation has to do with feelings? How children feel about something will determine what their attitudes are. If they have positive feelings about taking responsibility to do the right thing, they are well motivated. However, if they have negative feelings regarding taking responsibility, they are poorly motivated. Therefore, we need to train our children so that they will feel good about doing and being what is right and good.

My wife is the most positively motivated person I know. Pat is highly motivated in essentially all the right ways. It makes her feel good to help someone, to serve people, to carry out responsibilities, to accomplish projects. She can be depended on to come through and do a fantastic job in whatever she takes on. This is why she is so sought after to be on committees, boards, and in other areas of leadership, such as teaching and counseling. Pat's desire and motivation to function well comes from within. She does not wait to the last minute or depend on pressure to get her moving. She is able to do things well because accomplishing them is a pleasant experience for her.

I, on the other hand, am not self-motivated in the wonderful way Pat is. I have to be pressured to begin something, and then I often don't enjoy it because the pressure makes me feel anxious. I worry that I will not do a good job. This puts even more pressure on me.

Fortunately, our three children have become motivated in the same ways Pat is. Life is so much more enjoyable for those who have pleasant feelings when faced with life's responsibilities. But for those who have difficulty in prompting themselves to carry out their obligations, life is more of a burden. This is all too common today, with a majority of people having a difficult time meeting their obligations because they have been motivated in childhood with excessive pressure, rewards, threats, punishment, or guilt. They have never been taught to be motivated for the simple joy of feeling good about a job well done, or about pleasing or helping someone else. Instead, they respond to motivations that are selfish and self-serving.

One great difference between these two types of people is their level of optimism. In his book *Emotional Intelligence,* Daniel Goleman has this to say about optimism:

> Optimism, like hope, means having a strong expectation that, in general, things will turn out all right in life, despite setbacks and frustrations. From the standpoint of emotional intelligence, optimism is an attitude that buffers people against falling into apathy, hopelessness, or depression in the face of tough going. And, as with hope, its near cousin, optimism pays dividends in life (providing, of course, it is a realistic optimism; a too-naïve optimism can be disastrous).
>
> People who are optimistic see a failure as due to something that can be changed so that they can succeed next time around, while pessimists take the blame for failure, ascribing it to some lasting characteristic they are helpless to change.[1]

Goleman says that although one cause of a positive or negative outlook on life may be temperament, experience has a great contribution to the way we view life. We can learn to be optimistic as we become competent in challenges we take on. "People's beliefs about their abilities have a profound effect on those abilities. . . .

People who have a sense of self-efficacy bounce back from failures; they approach things in terms of how to handle them rather than worrying about what can go wrong."[2]

MOTIVATING BY EXAMPLE

Because life experiences have such power in motivating us, the setting in which children are raised has a profound effect. As parents, you are the primary factor in that setting. The way you deal with your own life issues is a powerful way to teach your children to be well motivated.

I have found that most people tend to look at motivation as they do child rearing: they believe that the way they are motivated is the best way and they try to pass it along to their children. Because you want your children to be positively motivated, it is important that you realize that your way may not be the best way. Whatever your own experience in the past, whatever your temperament, you will desire to present to your children an example of trustworthiness and honor, in the manner in which you meet your obligations. If they see you as a relaxed, uplifting, dedicated, pleasant, and consistent person, they will want to become like you. If they see you complaining and putting off your duties as long as possible, they will likely follow that example.

Because your example is so powerful to your children, you will want to strengthen it by doing the one thing that will, above all, cause your children to follow that example—communicating your constant love to them. The more they feel your unconditional love, the more they will follow your example. As they are motivated by conscious and positive examples of life experience, the less they will be motivated by negative subconscious motivations.

For many years I worked with the Head Start program, showing the teachers how to keep the children's emotional tanks full. Often a teacher would show me a three-year-old who was suffering from anxiety and fear resulting from emotional deprivation. I would ask the teacher first to teach the child something while sitting across the table from him. Then, I would ask her to teach something while holding the child and making occasional eye contact with him. Without fail, the child would show more attention when held. He understood better and seemed to learn more. What happened? The child could learn better when his emotional needs were cared for. Meeting these needs first eased the child's fears and anxiety and increased his sense of security and confidence. This enabled the child to learn better.

If this could happen in a short contact with a teacher, imagine how much more it can take place in the home with a loving parent.

SUBCONSCIOUS MOTIVATION AND VIOLENCE

The school shootings in the late nineties have alarmed me, but what has disturbed me equally is that no one I hear discussing it seems to understand this kind of tragedy. Even some mental health professionals are drawing everything out of the hat and blaming parents, guns, peer rejection, gangs, and violence—violence on television and the Internet, in movies and in music. This doesn't make sense to me. Japan and Hong Kong have far more violence in their media than we do. Many kids have much worse environments and parents than some of those doing the shootings. Even school security officials said that many other youngsters were far more worrisome and troublesome than the perpetrators. So, what is the answer?

While all of the alleged causes are certainly part of the overall problem, the underlying cause that provides the ignition is *subconscious motivation;* in this case, anger. The key to understanding the workings in the minds of the shooters is to understand how developing young minds handle anger, and how, without proper training in anger management, disaster will eventually result. For the first time in our history, we have reached the critical mass of negative influences without the counterbalance of shared positive values in our society.

Parents need to realize that they are the best influence to train their children in the handling of anger. Those who committed violent acts in public schools in Colorado, Oregon, Arkansas, and other places were apparently molded by evil influences and were not trained to control their anger in a mature way. As adolescents, they were naturally in their normal passive-aggressive stages and acted out their anger in a primitive and passive-aggressive manner. Yet, on the surface they appeared to be normal enough that no one was sufficiently suspicious to do anything about it.

Some of the kids who look weird and act strangely are acting out their passive-aggressive impulses in these ways. Those who did the shootings were keeping their anger hidden, to some extent even from themselves. This means that they were not consciously motivated but subconsciously. A person must be subconsciously driven to carry out acts as abnormal as these. Such barbarism requires the irrational and illogical reasoning of subconscious anger. If we do not learn to understand the complexity of these subconscious motivations, we will never be able as a society to effectively deal with them.

CONTROLLING A CHILD'S BEHAVIOR

In chapter 4, we talked about five ways to control behavior. Two of those are positive, two negative, and one neutral. It is important to remember this because pleasant feelings are the healthiest motivators—if the pleasant feelings are moving in the direction of guiding the child to do what is right. For this reason, training should be as positive and pleasant as possible. And also for this reason, punishment should not be the primary means of relating to a child.

This important concept of using positive means to control your child's behavior is exactly the opposite of what is being taught from some Christian sources today. If you relate to your child in primarily negative ways, such as corporal punishment, then your child will eventually develop subconscious motivations to do just the opposite of what you are trying to teach. However, if you use primarily positive ways to relate to and train your child, he will subconsciously desire to please you. He is receiving positive subconscious motivation.

How I wish all parents understood this! This lack of understanding is one of the primary reasons some of the best people in advantaged homes are producing children with some of the worst problems. I sometimes get discouraged from seeing so many children from seemingly good Christian homes who have developed serious, life-ruining problems. Their parents are usually well-meaning people who have been influenced by Christian books and speakers to employ reactive parenting. They have been persuaded to use negative means to control their children's behavior and have failed to meet their children's emotional needs first.

Reactive parenting produces several types of negative subconscious motivation, including passive-aggressive behavior. This anti-parent, antiauthority, anti-God attitude almost always results from this type of parenting. In the vast majority of cases, the parents are never able to understand why such a tragedy has happened in their home. They raised their children as they were taught to by Christian "experts." The children seemed to do well during their early years when primarily disciplinary approaches were used; but they turned against legitimate authority as they grew older.

Reactive parenting has had crushing consequences among Christian families today. Misunderstanding the true needs of their children, reactive parents have gone along with harsh, discipline-oriented parenting and then later watched their children develop anti-parent, antiauthority, anti-God attitudes and values.

CONTROLLING BEHAVIOR AND MOTIVATION

Because subconscious motivation is influenced largely by how we relate to our children, let's look again at the five ways to control a child's behavior, discussed in chapter 4. This time let's consider training and discipline in relation to motivation.

- Requests are the most positive means to control behavior. They lessen a child's anger and provide positive feelings within the child. A request says, "I respect the fact that you have feelings about this." A request also says, "I respect that you have opinions about this matter." And, best of all, it tells the child, "I am asking you to do this because I expect you to take responsibility for your own behavior." As you provide this kind of foundation, you are helping your child mature emotionally and psychologically. And you are giving your child that priceless attribute that is so missing in our culture today—taking responsibility for one's own behavior.

- Commands are negative means of controlling behavior. Yes, commands must be used at times, when requests fail, but it is important to remember that their verbal messages are negative. Commands usually elicit anger in a child because they suggest, "I don't care about your feelings or opinions in this matter. And I do not expect you to take responsibility for your own behavior here. I simply expect you to do what I tell you." All of this can rouse long-standing resentment in the child, since there is no love or emotional support involved. A constant diet of commands will fail to produce a mature person, especially in terms of motivation. Parents who find themselves constantly employing commands need to determine why their children are not responding to requests. The first place to look is the children's emotional tanks.

- Gentle physical manipulation is the other positive means to control a child's behavior. This means gently taking the child physically and moving him to do what you want him to do. If done with care, this will not create the negative feelings that commands and punishment usually do. Physical manipulation is especially effective with young children. However, it also can be used beautifully with an older child. For example, a young teenager may become so upset about something that it is best to remove him from a room where others are, to allow him to calm down before you take further action. You want to remove him graciously. Moving a child graciously from a room typically means you may take him by the arm or shoulder, or perhaps put your arm around him, and lead him in the direction you want him to go. As you gently move him, you might say, "Let's go over here and sit down for a few minutes." If your child has been raised with ample loving physical contact and is accustomed to touch, a situation like this can be handled well with such gentle physical manipulation. Once in the other room, you can deal with whatever upset him.

- Punishment is the most negative means of controlling behavior. If administered in a manner that is either too lenient or too permissive, the child's motivation will be negatively influenced. She will fail to develop an understanding of consequences and will be poorly motivated to do what is right. If the punishment is too severe, she will resent it and will probably develop antiauthority attitudes. This lessens the possibility that the parents will be able to provide positive motivation in the future.

- Behavior modification is a means of control that should be used sparingly. Frequent use of it centers the child's attention on rewards, on "What's in it for me?" We see this attitude today in young people who seem to want something for nothing and expect rewards for any effort, however small. Parents should use behavior modification appropriately and rarely.

NEGATIVE SUBCONSCIOUS MOTIVATIONS

It takes energy to be motivated. If most or all of a child's energy is needlessly used to cope with negative subconscious motivations, he will be poorly motivated and will have little energy left for positive motivations that lead to accomplishment. However, if a child is not burdened with using his energy to deal with negative subconscious motivations, he is free to develop into the person he was meant to be. When parents give their child what he needs emotionally, he can become positively motivated to want to please legitimate authority, to help others, to do what is right, and to be a good citizen. He also will desire to be a person of good morals and integrity, and to become a loving, caring, and Christlike Christian.

With all these positive results, it would seem parents would focus on giving positive motivations. The sad truth is that many parents contribute to the formation of subconscious negative motivations in their children. We need to look at four of the most common negative motivations.

Passive Aggression

Passive aggression is the worst subconscious motivation a person can have. It sets an undercurrent for almost all other motivations. Regardless of what the person's ambitions and dreams are, the passive-aggressive way of handling anger will work directly against them. I believe this to be the greatest potential hindrance in anyone's life.

Need to Prove One's Worth

When a child feels the need to prove her worth in order to earn her parents' love, she is in a deplorable and pitiable situation. Many children never do satisfy the hunger in their hearts for parental love and approval, no matter how long they live.

The tragedy is that most of those parents actually do love their children, but they never are able to transmit that love to the hearts of their children. One reason is that they have never loved their children unconditionally and have never met their emotional needs. Lacking this critical foundation, these children spend the rest of their lives being controlled by negative and harmful emotions.

Guilt

Guilt as a negative subconscious motivation is a special hazard for parents of shy, reticent, and easy-to-handle children. These pliable kids are easy to control because they have a deep need to please. If they don't think that they are pleasing authority figures, they feel inadequate and guilty. It is easy for parents to pick up on this and inadvertently use guilt as a way to control them.

This is a serious mistake, for the children will develop no motivations other than to defend themselves against the dreaded feelings of guilt. This makes them easy prey to stronger-minded and controlling persons. Eventually such children can become weak-minded, easily influenced, and unable to think for themselves. This can make them subject to evil influences and to suggestions of wrongdoing. Their need to please can prevent them from becoming self-sufficient and independent persons.

If your children desire to please and can easily feel inadequate, be careful. Your challenge is to provide these children with a sense of security based on love and approval. Then they can develop their naturally wonderful traits of caring and compassion, and they will want to do what is right.

Pressure

Pressure is another form of negative motivation that is sometimes unconscious, sometimes conscious. Parents can easily use pressure to get their children to do what they want. At times this may be necessary, but be careful. Such pressure can be harmful.

Pressure means using threatening means to get children to perform. This may be done through *disapproval,* especially harmful to sensitive and approval-seeking children; *anger,* which is almost always a mistake; or *punishment or threat of punishment,* which produces anxiety and fear in the children. Anxiety and fear are poor motivators because they cause children to become ineffective or even paralyzed.

Parents who overuse pressure actually harm their child's ability to accomplish what they want him to do. One of the greatest problems people have in performing certain activities is anxiety. Parents will not want to add to a child's level of anxiety by continually exerting pressure.

PREPARING A CHILD TO LEARN

Children are born with an innate hunger for learning that remains strong—unless adults bore, spank, overly pressure, or otherwise discourage it out of them. If you carefully observe young children at play, you discover that they are almost constantly working to learn new skills. At each stage, one of their primary ways of learning is to imitate adults. The activity they like the best is the one in which they are learning something new. Normally, your child *wants* to learn. The motivation is already there.

Though children already desire to learn, parents and teachers need to remember this important principle of learning: *For a child to be able to learn well, he must be at the emotional maturational level of his particular age level.* Emotional maturity means the ability to control anxiety, withstand stress, and maintain balance during times of change.

Children who are starved for love and acceptance from their parents will have little motivation to accept the challenges of learning. If they are distressed with anxiety or melancholy, or if they feel unloved, they most likely will have problems with concentration and attention span, and will feel a decrease in energy. They will definitely be less motivated, especially in subjects in which they have less initial interest.

As parents we have the greatest part in seeing that our children are ready to learn. We do this by keeping their emotional tanks full and lovingly training them. Children who are doing well emotionally will have the concentration, motivation, and energy they need to use their abilities to the maximum. It is critical that we bring our children to emotional maturity and not let them fall behind.

MOTIVATING YOUR CHILD
TO TAKE RESPONSIBILITY FOR SCHOOLWORK

To help you determine when you can expect a child to take responsibility for himself, you need to remind yourself of this simple truth: *Two persons cannot take responsibility for the same thing at the same time.* When you take responsibility for something, the child is unable to. Your child cannot take the responsibility until you allow him to. As your child grows, you want to let him take on that challenge, little by little, as it is appropriate to his age and ability.

Homework presents a classic challenge for most families. As long as you take the responsibility for the homework, your child cannot and will not. As a result, she will not learn to take the initiative. One secret in motivating a child, and keeping her motivated, is to allow her to take the initiative. Part of the training process with a child is to gradually move away from taking all responsibility and initiative to allowing the child to take this for herself. *When the child is taking the initiative, she is taking responsibility. When she takes responsibility, she is motivated.*

Most children have periods of time when they resist doing their homework. This is especially true in that one normal passive-aggressive period during the early teenage years. Even during this difficult stage, you need to realize that the homework is your child's responsibility. You can mention that you will be happy to help with the homework if he asks you. Then, when he asks, you need to avoid taking any of the work on yourself and place it right back on your child's shoulders.

For instance, if your child has a math problem and asks you for help, you can look at the math book, find where it covers that type of problem, and then hand the book back and say something like this, "It tells how to do that type of problem on this page. See if that helps and let me know. I'll be right here." When you continue to refer your child to the source where he can find the answer himself, you are teaching him initiative, responsibility, self-reliance, and motivation. You can also suggest that he ask the teacher for more explanation, if that is necessary.

If you have been too involved in your child's homework and now wish to shift responsibility to her, you may see a brief drop in grades. However, your child's ability to assume responsibility and to become self-reliant will serve her well for the rest of her life. As she requires less and less help from you, the two of you can spend some of your time together exploring other areas of special interest to you both.

Highly motivated people who take initiative and responsibility for their own behavior are in short supply today. What a wonderful gift to leave with your children—the ability to be self-sufficient, rather than having to depend on others for what they should be able to do for themselves. Most children are placed in a position where parents and teachers take the initiative and then assume responsibility for their learning. Adults do this because they genuinely care for the children and mistakenly believe that they should be doing more for them.

Of course, normal children are eventually going to rebel against this type of control. As parents, we must aid our children to progress from our control to self-control as their maturity develops. While we don't want to rush this process, giving too much responsibility before children have the skill and judgment to manage it well, we don't want to make the mistake of unnecessary delay. When parents assume too much control, we rob our children of creativity and enthusiasm and their natural desire to learn.

MOTIVATING YOUR CHILD IN SPECIAL INTERESTS

In chapter 8 we described new findings on brain development in children and teenagers. This has special application to exposing your children to new activities. Children want to try new things. The challenge for parents is to help their children find wholesome sources of stimulation. And, for some, one challenge may be to pry them away from the television. Jay Giedd, a child psychiatrist at the National Institute of Mental Health in Betheseda, Maryland, has said:

> Teenagers are choosing what their brains are going to be good at—learning right from wrong, responsibility or impulsiveness, thinking or video games. . . . This argues for doing a lot of things as a teenager. You are hard-wiring your brain in adolescence. Do you want to hard-wire it for sports and playing music and doing mathematics—or for lying on the couch in front of the television?[3]

How often we hear people lament that they didn't continue taking music lessons when they were young. They say, "I wish my parents had made me stay with it." And yet, as so many parents know, forcing a child to do something he is determined to quit is a senseless battle. Just how do you motivate a child to a long-term involvement?

Assume for now that the interest you want your child to pursue is the piano; you need to be both patient and clever about whetting his appetite. You want him to take the initiative. This means that you need to provide an exposure to piano music and to people who play. Let your child develop a desire to play and then wait until he asks to take lessons. Better yet, stall until he is begging you to study piano.

Once your child wants to study piano, you can act as if you are doing a huge favor—which you really are—and give in to his request. This is the time to obtain promises of commitment from your child to practice and to be dedicated to learning. Then later, when his enthusiasm wanes, you can gently remind him of his promises to carry through with the commitment.

This is the only sure way to persuade a child to take on a long-term commitment—to let him take the initiative and the responsibility first. If you take the initiative, you are also taking the responsibility, and in the long run, the child probably will not. Once your child has taken the initiative and begins lessons, you are in a great position. Then, your encouragement and praise are truly meaningful. Your child feels that you are supporting him, not just trying to get him to do something that you want.

It is wise to give your child opportunities to acquire healthy interests and to have a curiosity about activities that can have lifelong benefits. Once your daughter shows interest and takes initiative, you have her hooked. It is not your thing anymore, for it belongs to her. Pushing your child into something, and then using pressure to keep her going, almost never works.

What you need to offer is encouragement.

As your child develops his or her interest, be careful to avoid excessive praise. Too much praise can come across to the child as the parent taking the responsibility, and you know what that will do: The child will take less responsibility, especially as she becomes older. Also, the people-pleasing child can actually come to feel dependent on the praise when she is small, and have a difficult time when she doesn't get enough of it. Then, as she grows older, she may come to gradually resent the praise and consider the undertaking "my parent's thing." It needs to be "my thing" to the child. Praise should be used with discretion so that it will mean something to the child over the years.

Offering rewards can present the same problem. Rewards can be quite effective when used occasionally for special reasons. But, if they are used routinely, they will lose their effectiveness. As the child comes to expect the reward, she will no longer be motivated by it.

As you look at your style of parenting, you may find that you are not providing enough stimulation for your children to reach into many interests and have an enriched life. Or you may find that you have been doing too much for your children, thus discouraging them from taking initiative and responsibility for themselves.

Clearly, motivating our children takes knowledge and effort, especially in these difficult days. I earnestly hope that you will put into practice what we have talked about in this chapter. You will need to review these concepts to learn the art of producing well-motivated children, but you can certainly do it.

The rewards of motivating your children—to learn, to accomplish projects, to serve others—are tremendous. With proper motivation, your children will avoid many struggles, and they will develop an edge in life that will continue to serve them well.

NOTES

1. Daniel Goleman, *Emotional Intelligence* (New York: Bantam Books, 1995), 88.
2. Ibid., 90.
3. Shannon Brownlee, "Inside the Teen Brain," *U.S. News & World Report*, 9 August 1999, 47, 53.

Chapter Eleven

Questions and Answers About Being a Proactive Parent

During the many years I have been involved in counseling families, I have seen countless parents helped by a proactive approach in dealing with their children. They have discovered renewed and growing joy in their relationships within their families.

I have received many questions from fathers and mothers who wonder how to become more proactive and relational in their parenting. Here are some of the most common ones. Perhaps similar questions have popped into your mind as you have read this book.

I hope the answers will be helpful as you seek to form deep and meaningful relationships within your family circle. The answers will point you to positive, relational parenting, the kind that will prepare your children for responsible adult living.

1. *You say that physical touch should be maintained during the child's teen years, but my son really seems uncomfortable*

with my touching him. Can you give me some suggestions on how I can maintain touching in the next few years? I'm stumped.

Ross: Look for every opportunity to make physical contact with your teenage son (or daughter), even if the teen seems withdrawn. Here are a few instances when it is easiest to make physical contact with any teenager:

> - When something funny is happening, like a joke or a funny TV program. Touch him on the leg as you laugh together; clasp her on the arm as you groan and comment.
> - When the teenager is upset and wants comfort.
> - When you have something important to tell her. Perhaps a peer is on the phone, a call she has been waiting for. Instead of yelling at her, tap her on the shoulder, smile, and give a thumbs up of support.
> - When you can raise an everyday event to a level of importance in the child's eyes. You might accompany it with a pat on the back or a high-five or quick hug—whatever is appropriate for the age and gender of your child.
> - When you can distract him. For example, when an unusual car is passing by, you can point out the car and at the same time place your hand gently on his arm. Or when you are passing in a hallway, you can make natural physical contact.

It is not difficult to find ways to make natural physical contact with a teenager. Remember, it doesn't matter if he is aware of the touch, because it goes through the same neural pathways in his brain to his hypothalamus anyway, whether he is conscious of the touch or not. Over time, he will recall those touches and appreciate them (even if he doesn't say so).

2. *You say that parents should try to avoid the punishment trap. To do this, you suggest sitting down with a spouse or good friend to decide on right punishments for various offenses. Shouldn't the child have a say in the decision?*

ROSS: When your child is young and/or too immature to objectively make such a decision, it would be inappropriate to let the child determine punishment. However, your child will progress in his ability to think objectively and eventually will be able to understand the reasoning behind punishment, as well as the importance of punishment being appropriate to the offense. As he does so, he may be allowed gradually to participate in making this kind of decision. As parents, you must always retain authority to make the final decision.

As your child moves into the teenage years, discipline and training need to gradually change from a basis of parental control to one of parental trust. Privileges and freedom should depend on the child's trustworthiness. When your child is young, you take most of the responsibility in determining his behavior. But as he becomes a preadolescent, beginning to experience the drive for independence, he will attempt to exert more control and to make decisions about his actions. As parents, you need to work to make this transition as smooth as possible.

The degree to which you can trust your child and his ability to control his behavior is the best indicator you have in determining how much say-so you will give your child in making decisions, including the consequences for his behavior. Please read my book *How to Really Love Your Teenager* for a more complete discussion of this vital topic.

3. *Why do you think so many parents fall into the punishment trap?*

ROSS: One reason is that so many books, articles, seminars, radio programs, and sermons advocate corporal punishment, even while they gloss over or bypass all the other needs of the child, especially for love.

Few today are pleading for a child, and many are dogmatically calling for children to be immediately punished for misbehavior. They call this discipline and recommend harsh forms of treatment as the answer to the problems of today's youth.

As noted in chapter 4, key Scriptures are being misused, particularly Proverbs 29:15. Let's remember that the rod was primarily an instrument of comfort and guidance (Psalm 23:4), not chastisement.

Finally, these advocates of corporal punishment rarely say that there are times when punishment can be harmful. Many parents come away from lectures and seminars with the idea that corporal punishment is the primary or even the only way to relate to their children. This is sad.

4. *You say that parents have so much power and authority available. How can they show meekness in their responses and yet maintain their authority?*

ROSS: Meekness is not weakness. It is using your authority and power in mature ways. Meekness continually exercises its authority with loving concern for the children's best interests. To be meek is not to be permissive. As a parent you always need to be in control.

Jesus used His power to care for others, not to vent His own displeasure or display His authority. Wisely making meekness a part of parenting will hold us on a loving path with our children; and it will keep us from misusing our parental power and falling into the punishment trap.

When you are angry but restrain yourself from talking in an unpleasant way or yelling, you are displaying meekness. Remain pleasant but firm when you display your power. Maintaining your self-control and refusing to dump your anger on your children are part of practicing meekness.

Over the years, our attitude of meekness will save us heartaches and pain as our precious ones reach adolescence. That's particularly true when our children have observed in us something of this Christlike attitude. Once they are teenagers, you will no longer have the degree of controlling power and authority you had when they were young. Then you must rely increasingly on your relationship of love and trust. If you have shown meekness when they were younger, you will enjoy the results during their teenage years.

5. *In the maze of advice from so many quarters, how can we know if we are following the right course in raising our children?*

ROSS: You can know whether you are on the right track by looking at your motives and your priorities, as well as the atmosphere in your home. You want to have the most positive and pleasant and loving relationship with your children as possible. At the same time, you want them to develop self-control and to learn to act appropriately.

In order to see these two vital happenings in your children's lives, you must give them two things. First, give them unconditional love, and give it appropriately. Second, give your children loving discipline, that is, training in the most positive way possible. Train by all available means, doing so in ways that enhance the self-esteem of your children and that do not demean or hurt them. *Positive guidance to good behavior is far superior to negative punishment for poor behavior.*

If you find that your interaction with your children is primarily negative, centered on their poor behavior, you will know that you need to make some changes in the overall approach and atmosphere in your home. Parenting that is primarily negative and punitive is going to produce negative results. I know that this is not what you want for your children.

Your children want to identify with you. Make that easy and inviting for them with largely positive interactions with them.

6. *I wish you would explain more about the anger ladder. Do you mean that when I reach the top rung—being pleasant, seeking resolution—I am expressing my anger the right way? Should my eighteen-year-old ideally be at the top of the ladder?*

ROSS: The anger ladder is a visual illustration of highly complex ways we can behave when angry. Managing one's anger is a difficult and lifelong process, one that none of us does perfectly. It is therefore important that we are continually moving upward in our ability to handle our anger in a mature fashion.

When I say that I expected my own children to be able to handle anger maturely by age seventeen, that means that I expected them to be able to manage themselves generally in a pleasant verbal manner, instead of in an unpleasant and behavioral manner. That does not mean that they were able to do this all the time but that a mature pattern had been established in anger management, one that they could build on in the future.

7. *Is televised violence really that damaging to a child? Doesn't he know the difference between fantasy and reality?*

ROSS: In the summer of 1999, the NBC newsmagazine *Dateline* reported the story of four teenage boys living in a Florida community. At school and home they had seemed to be fairly normal kids, but the four had banded together as "The Lords of Chaos" and perpetrated several acts of violence in their town. After arson, vandalism, and burglary, they murdered a teacher from their high school.

Now, five years later, two of the boys were being interviewed by NBC. It soon was clear in the interview that they had not been distinguishing adequately between fantasy and reality. They were acting out something similar to what they saw regularly on television and in videos.

In chapter 7, I described a presentation by David Walsh, which showed the effects of having young children watch TV programming. Walsh presented videos of Barney to young children, and then of the Power Rangers. After each video, the children imitated what they had seen. Their watching parents were first amused and then horrified at what was happening. This demonstration took just a few minutes. Imagine the influence on children who watch violent programs and videos on a regular basis.

According to the National Coalition on Television Violence, on the average, each child in our country will watch at least 200,000 violent acts before the age of eighteen. A *TV Guide* study found that the average American child will be exposed to approximately 45,000 sexual messages in their early years.[1] This data is from an excellent book by David Walsh, *Selling Out America's Children*. I strongly urge you to read his insightful and challenging book.

8. *The Internet offers lots of great family web sites as well as important information for children and teenagers. Yet I can't always monitor everything they watch. So how can I protect them from unwanted and dangerous web sites?*

Ross: First, consider applying the suggestions I made in chapter 7 about the control of TV viewing to Internet watching. Also, consider placing the computer in a central area where it will be accessible to everyone.

Next, think about installing software filters that screen content. When CNET's SmutBusters tested several blockers and evaluated their ability to filter inappropriate material, they found Cyber Patrol to be the best overall web site blocker. These filters are software programs you insert in your computer.

The main drawback of this system is that it is somewhat complicated to set up. However, its positives outnumber the negatives. For instance, you can configure as many as nine users, set the hours during which each can access the Internet, block the typing of specific words—such as names and addresses, so that your kids don't become vulnerable during a chat to those seeking direct contact—and restrict access to risqué news groups. If you share the computer with kids of many ages, Cyber Patrol is excellent at personalizing many options. The phone number is 800-828-2608.

You may also want to consider Internet providers that offer access to the Net and are also able to do the screening for you. My wife, Pat, was using America Online one day when she began receiving pornography through E-mail. If this happened to her, you can imagine how many children have been exposed to this type of material simply by having an E-mail address. One provider that will screen the web sites for you is Rated-G Online. The address is www.ratedg.com.

9. *You said that when your children's friends were asked to name their favorite hangout during their high school days, your house was rated second after a local eating place. What did you do to make your home a comfortable place for your teenage children and their friends? What other activities would you recommend that would make teens want to invite friends over, and yet would not include TV or video watching?*

ROSS: My wife and I began planning early for our children's adolescent days, fixing up our older home to provide a space to which our children would want to bring their friends. We furnished the family room with such games as ping pong and pool.

As our children grew, I tried to take the time to get to know their friends and their parents. We wanted to learn everything we could about them and their problems. This was easy to do with the kids who went to our church, but we had to find other ways to get to know the other kids; we did this mainly through ball teams and school functions.

When the adolescent years arrived, we let our kids know that we would love to have their friends over whenever possible. We made them welcome by providing meals after games and other special events. Whenever we had opportunity, we would talk to each teen individually. When we showed interest in their lives, they would tell us more and more about themselves. Even today, most of them visit with us whenever they are in town. Many of them send us their annual newsletters with personal notes to keep us informed. We have enjoyed the friendships of our children's friends.

The way you make your own home a refuge for your children and their friends may differ from ours. Be creative, but be sure your children are comfortable entertaining others at your home. And be involved. Making friends with their friends lets those friends know you care about your children's welfare and theirs.

10. *You say that a child who is starved for love and acceptance from his or her parents "will have little motivation to accept the challenges of learning." Won't a child with a high IQ or great curiosity still learn? What difference will love make in his ability to learn?*

Ross: Every child has emotional needs. Especially the need for unconditional love must be fulfilled in order for the child to learn well. An IQ is not a fixed item. As a child grows and matures intellectually, she can fall behind with decreasing IQ unless she is properly nourished emotionally. A child also grows and matures emotionally. If she is not nourished emotionally, she can fall behind and become an immature person.

Curiosity is similar, for a child's curiosity will shrivel up and die if there is insufficient emotional nurture. One reason for this is that curiosity takes emotional energy which, if not supplied through emotional nurture, will not be sufficient to enable the child to maintain interest. Second, the lack of adequate emotional nurture causes a child to feel unloved and inadequate. This, in turn, produces such problems as depression, anxiety, and poor self-esteem. And those problems can lead to low energy, poor concentration, distractibility, and decreased memory—all problems that interfere with learning.

In short, a child's emotional health is just as important as her innate IQ when it comes to her ability to learn.

11. *How does a child's emotional health affect learning in the school setting?*

ROSS: I wish more school administrators understood the importance of emotional health in a child. Teachers certainly do. They are required to teach children who are not ready to learn because of emotional deprivation and cannot learn on their age or grade level. Worse yet, emotional immaturity causes misbehavior and antiauthority attitudes. Working in these impossible situations leaves teachers discouraged and waiting for retirement.

We must find ways to help our teachers maintain good morale. They are our best hope for children who have been deprived of love and nurture at home. Of course, we need to also assist parents to meet this critical challenge of properly caring for their children, but it is more feasible to assist our teachers first. They are already dedicated to helping children. The vast majority of teachers are highly motivated people. I find it sad to see the ways their superiors in many school systems are discouraging and demoralizing them. Often parents are failing to prepare their children emotionally for school, yet the teachers are receiving the blame and feeling the pressure to produce educational results in children who are not ready to learn at their age level.

We need to support our teachers whenever possible. In this way we are helping our precious children.

12. *Can you suggest positive ways to use the media?*

ROSS: There are still many good programs on television, and many good movies appear on TV, both newly made and those from years ago, including classic black and white films. The key is to make those available to children during times when they are able to watch. I suggest using the VCR to record good programs or movies. I especially like TV shows that offer an ethical or moral lesson—like the old Andy Griffith Show. Many of the older programs deal with life issues in positive ways.

A dear friend of ours, Fredrica, is a second-grade teacher in Pensacola, Florida. She recently told us this revealing and touching story. One of her students, a seven-year-old girl, had exceptional good manners and was considerate of adults and other children. She was caring and cooperative in every way.

One day Fredrica said to this girl, "You have such nice manners. You must come from a family that teaches wonderful manners." The little girl answered, "No, I try to get my manners from black and white movies."

When Fredrica asked her what she meant, the child explained that she liked the way people treated each other in the older movies and she tried to treat other people that way. Fredrica was astounded that such a young child would be so positively affected by old black and white films. Yes, movies and television programs, properly chosen, can have a positive effect on our children.

13. *What is the value of parents playing with children?*

ROSS: Having times of laughter, excitement, and fun with our children is fantastic. We share experiences, create memories, and bond together.

Playing with my kids has real meaning for me. How I yearn for the days when I played ball with my sons and daughter, went river rafting with them, or played indoor games on a rainy day. What joy we shared and how they grew in depth, even at those moments when they lost their cool because they were too tired or didn't win the game.

All of us look back on our times of playing together with fondness. Because we played then, we are still able to play together now, when they are all grown and our family circle is enlarging.

NOTE

1. David Walsh, *Selling Out America's Children* (Minneapolis: Fairview Press, 1994), 52.

Epilogue

Christian hope does not depend on what the world does to us. It depends on what we do in the world, as we live in response to God's great love for us. Sometimes I can almost see Jesus Christ looking down and cheering us on, along with so many believers of ages past (those described in Hebrews 12:1).

This is exactly what our children need us to do for them. We are to be their supporters, cheering their every effort. This is the message of proactive parenting. We are cheerleaders; we are advocates. One of the most critical findings of a 1999 study by Barna Research concerned what children said they wanted for themselves.[1] The first item was unconditional love. They wanted parents who always supported them.

The children expressed this need for unconditional love in various phrases:

> "Being loved regardless of what I do"
> "Feeling connected to my parents"
> "Feeling that my parents accept me for who I am"

The second thing that children wanted was better communication with their parents. This included a deeper interaction, and not so much time spent on superficial matters. Third, they desired a greater amount of time with their parents. They rarely received the focused attention that they needed.

The kids in the study also expressed their need for respect from their parents. Children have a deep craving for personal dignity, and this has to come first from parents.

Fifth, they indicated their need for a sense of purpose and meaning in life. Young people today are looking for spiritual meaning, and this leads them to explore in many different directions.

Significantly, those five desires imply that we give our children an unconditional love and a purpose for living.

In addition, children who participated in the Barna survey said that they wanted to be closer emotionally to their families. They felt isolated from other family members and needed a greater sense of unity, security, and understanding. They wanted to experience greater loyalty within the family unit.

The greatest fear of many young people, according to the Barna study, is that their parents will divorce. They desire to see their parents express deeper respect and love for each other. Some children are plagued with concerns of violence, poverty, and abandonment. Most are living with some kind of pain and fear that relates to their parents and other family members.

You may never know how your children would respond to such questions. But you can make sure that you provide the kind of home and personal relationships that will satisfy your children's deepest needs and ensure an adequate foundation for the future, when they will leave our homes and enter the world as adults.

The goal is to release our children as mature adults. However, letting our children go is not something that happens only when they are eighteen (or twenty-one). It happens little by little. The way we deal with our total training and also our gradual releasing of our children will make all the difference between pain and joy. For the releasing, just as the training, depends heavily on the deep expression of love we are offering to our children day by day.

Whenever they leave us, for a few hours, for a week at camp, for a semester at college, or to venture into the adult world, they should take with them the love and security we have implanted in their hearts. With this they can move into appropriate levels of maturity. As proactive parents, we prepare them for the future with the love, security, and encouragement we give as we raise them today.

Fellow parents, let's prepare them for that day they become mature adults. Let's be encouragers, dispensers of the hope that our children and teenagers so desperately need.

I guarantee that when you do this, when you cheer your children on to maturity, you'll find it is truly rewarding, for it is like giving water to a drought-parched earth. They will be able to blossom. And, as your children grow and flourish, they too will become cheerleaders, offering hope to others.

NOTE

1. George Barna, "Inward, Outward & Upward: Ministry That Transforms Lives," report of the Barna Research Group (Ventura, Calif.: 1999), 18–23.

Study Guide

CHAPTER ONE

1. How do forces outside yourself as a parent—that is, the schools, media, community, or even church—work against the values you are trying to teach your child? In what ways has this made your job as a parent more difficult?

2. Have you at times failed to explicitly communicate to your child the deep love you feel for him? And when you do communicate that love, why may he sometimes not receive it as you intend? What does this tell you about your relationship?

3. Based on your family upbringing, advice from others, or books you've read on the subject, which parenting style do you usually gravitate toward—reacting to behavior or providing for needs in a give-and-take relationship?

4. In Mary's story, her parents weren't aware that a fundamental need of their child was unmet. Look at the four foundation stones of effective parenting. Have any of these areas perhaps been given inadequate attention?

5. In which of the four areas do you do best? Is it because of your understanding of the need, your basic inclination to meet it, or both?

CHAPTER TWO

1. Regardless of your age as a parent, what do you remember in your past when society was more supportive of your parenting values? What might you need to change or add in today's parenting world to make up for this lack of support?

2. To what degree have you been influenced by the theories of behavior modification? What role has reinforcement of behavior played in your parenting techniques?

3. In light of the previous question, have rewards and punishments come before anticipating your child's emotional needs or previous motives? How can you better incorporate emotional nurturance in responding to your child?

4. Why do you think Christian children brought up in a conservative family, who have also made a personal commitment to Christ, engage in immoral behavior? Does this make you want to challenge your parenting assumptions?

5. Does this indicate to you that rewards and punishment incentives may later fail when children become teenagers or enter college? Why don't rewards or punishments alone produce good behavior?

CHAPTER THREE

1. Do you tend to love your children in ways that you think are best or in ways that mean more to them? Depending on their age, try to interact with them to find out how they feel loved. Then attempt to put those expressions into practice.

2. Why do you think that a foundation of unconditional love will keep you from being either too harsh or too lenient? Why will your child respect you more in terms of added discipline when this foundation is in place?

3. Work out a practical plan to exhibit love to your child unconditionally—that is, regardless of his behavior. Try to determine, by observing his general state of being, whether his emotional love tank is being filled. Review the positive qualities expressed in the chapter related to a full love tank.

4. Physical touch can be accomplished in many healthy ways and has a number of benefits for your child. Make a list of circumstances and opportunities, based upon your child's needs and sensitivities, to provide caring physical touch that expresses your love.

5. Eye contact and focused attention are related and critically important to your child's well-being. Make a new resolution to practice this. Also, rearrange the priorities on your calendar to spend time alone with your child and focus on his needs.

CHAPTER FOUR

1. Describe the different motivations behind being either too permissive or too controlling. What are the natures of the different fears attached to each approach? What might be the outcome of each extreme?

2. Though punishment may be the negative side of discipline, there are a number of positive forms the author mentions. Explain the greater value of the following: example, learning experiences, and verbal instructions. Make a plan to use these to a greater degree.

3. Think back to some of the hostility or supposed rebellion on the part of your child. Are these times that the root cause goes beyond simple disobedience to unmet needs? How can you better analyze this behavior in the future?

4. Do you often, as many parents do, give commands instead of requests? Do you feel at times that requests would undermine your authority? Why is meekness not weakness, and what positive results may come from requests rather than commands?

5. List both the positive and negative sides of spanking. In light of this, at what times has spanking been the best response in your past dealings with your child?

CHAPTER FIVE

1. Take a decision in your child's life that requires some thinking through to arrive at the right conclusion. Ask him to express his feelings about the decision, and help him arrive at the decision by using his own thinking process. Are the values and principles he is using correct?

2. How have you taught the concept of integrity to your child? Does he clearly understand the concepts of honesty, keeping his word, and taking responsibility? Make sure your child understands this in the practical areas of his everyday life.

3. Many of us supply answers and give commands but do not share with our children the mental process we use in teaching them. The next time you teach values, share the reasoning behind your position, and listen to (as well as answer) your child's views.

4. How can you better release your child to make his own decisions? Talk to him about consequences and the relationship between responsibility and privileges. How can you explain that your parental guidelines are really meant to hasten his independence?

5. Think back to some circumstances or events in the last week that could have led to a "teachable moment" for your child. Write down how those situations could have led to growth on the part of your child. What situations may arise in the coming week and how can you prepare yourself to teach?

CHAPTER SIX

1. What will happen if you refuse to allow your child to verbally express his anger, or in turn, dump your own anger on him? In what ways can you *positively* use his anger to help him grow toward maturity?

2. Define passive-aggressive behavior. Why is it so hard to detect and understand, and what is the major cause of it?

3. What is the best approach to your child's anger in order to avoid passive-aggressive behavior?

4. Measure your own success in dealing with your child's anger in the following three areas: not condemning him, focusing on what he did right, and helping him express his anger more positively. What can you learn here about your weakest areas?

5. To what extremes do you gravitate when your child gets angry? Do you tend to avoid conflict or get out of control with your own anger? How does this in turn lead to wrong reactions from your child? How do you stop this cycle?

CHAPTER SEVEN

1. Make a project of discovering your child's total media consumption, both in terms of time and content. Include TV, video games, computer, music, movies, and written material. What is your assessment of the value of the overall content and how it might affect your child?

2. What effects have television and movies had on your child's values or view of the world? Think of various programs, scenes, actors, etc., that have provoked positive or negative responses from your child. What does this say about the overall role of the media in your child's moral development?

3. Look at the list of suggestions on a wise use of television. Which of these would present viable alternatives to the harmful effects of television in the lives of your children? Make a commitment to introduce three of these options to your children in the next month.

4. If there is some disagreement over programs or movies, consider the possibility of watching with your children a questionable program that is borderline objectionable to you but more acceptable to them. How might you be able to discuss the contents and better understand each child's point of view?

5. Come up with a list of at least three books, videos, movies, or TV programs that you believe teach the values that you want to communicate to your child. Try to make these choices relate in some way to the world of your child. Then buy, rent, or borrow these items for the child, explaining why you like them and ask your child to read or watch them and then talk with you about them.

CHAPTER EIGHT

1. Why is it impossible to teach your child spiritually if you have not nurtured your child emotionally? Is it very likely that your child will discover the love of God if he hasn't been regularly affirmed by you? At the same time, how can you link your emotional nurturance with spiritual parallels?

2. What previous negative emotions or lack of certain positive emotions must your child deal with in order to better comprehend the wonderful truths of God's care for him? If possible, talk with your child about any possible obstacles related to his potential spiritual growth.

3. Share your own conversion and other spiritual experiences with your child at a level that he can handle. Demonstrate to him that God is the giver of all good things and that He is the foundation of your life. How can you make your experiences relevant to your child's desires and needs?

4. Your child should be made aware of what issues you are praying about for your own life and those around you. Do you share prayer requests with each other? Though this could be a difficult challenge, invite your child to pray with you regarding all your joint needs. Thank God for each other.

5. Is your child open to hearing about the Bible if you make it interesting? The Bible is very important in terms of offering your child comfort, joy, hope, and a host of other things. Share with him the many promises, prayers, stories, teaching, etc., that God has in store personally for him.

CHAPTER NINE

1. The author points out that some older parents are able through their experiences to help younger parents with difficult problems like teenage depression. Try to connect with more experienced parents and seek wisdom regarding issues related to your child that you don't fully understand.

2. Depression can be prevented in a home atmosphere that is laid-back, upbeat, peaceful, loving, and humorous. Which of these characteristics are often present in your home? How might each one's presence or absence affect your child's mood and self-assessment?

3. Define the difference between negative and positive anxiety. What are the downsides of each extreme? How can positive anxiety, or even positive stress, help your child?

4. Why is it often difficult to detect depression in children? Take a look at the extended list of symptoms in the chapter and even if you find slight evidence, consult with your spouse and your child for more details related to the combination of symptoms present in any degree. Might they signify even mild depression?

5. Keeping in mind the need for a positive atmosphere described earlier, what negative words, attitudes, and influences can be omitted from your home, and even beyond your home, to help minimize depression in your child? Try also to focus on what healthy things might challenge, excite, and please him based on his unique personality.

CHAPTER TEN

1. What is the general motivation level of your child? Is he energized and responsible, or does he complain and procrastinate? How would you describe both his aptitudes and attitudes combining to affect his overall response to his environment?

2. At times we misread what is really motivating us by not discerning the subconscious motivation involved. Begin by looking at yourself. Are there some less-than-praiseworthy motivations for good behavior or goals? Now discuss those of your child and help him work on proper motivation.

3. Why is it ironic that adults who in childhood seem to have received a more direct push to succeed, who've experienced pressure, rewards, threats, punishment, or guilt, have the most difficulty being motivated? How do all of the above sometimes act as hindrances to better performance? What ingredient was left out that works better?

4. Why is childhood emotional maturity—handling anxiety, stress, and change—actually necessary for mental activities such as learning? How does a lack of love or total acceptance affect things like concentration, attention span, and energy?

5. If your child is going to make a long-term commitment to anything worthwhile, he needs to take the initiative. What are some ways in which you can provide a conducive environment to allow this initiative to be born and grow? Be aware that he might initially resist something which in the long run fits his aptitudes and attitudes.

The Five Love Languages **just got a smaller vocabulary.**

The Five Love Languages of Children
Gary Chapman & Ross Campbell, M.D.
1-881273-65-2

Discover your child's primary love language!
Children are intricate and unique personalities.
Learn what you can do to effectively convey unconditional feelings of respect, affection, and commitment that will resonate in your child's
behaviors and emotions. *Key Best Seller*.

Parenting doesn't end at eighteen.

Parenting Your Adult Child
*How You Can Help Them Achieve
Their Full Potential*
Ross Campbell, M.D. & Gary Chapman
1-881273-12-1

Parenting no longer ends at eighteen, but there are few resources available to help parents communicate with their adult child. Covering topics such as When Adult Children Return Home and Religious Choices, this book is a unique tool for today's parents.

Strengthen your family's vital signs.

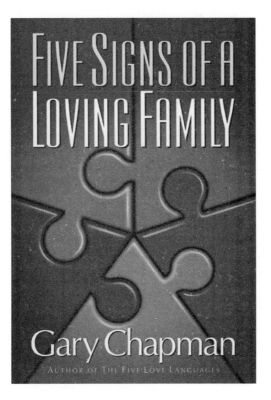

Five Signs of a Loving Family
Gary Chapman
1-881273-92-X

Take a look at what a truly successful family looks
like and how it functions. Depsite the problems
that are prevalent in today's society, you can make
the dream of healthy family relationships come
true.